Learn 33 Hit Songs On Guitar Just 3 Chords Per Song

For The Beginner To Advancing Guitarist

Author: Ged Brockie

Copyright © 2020 GMI - Guitar & Music Institute

www.guitarandmusicinstitute.com

ISBN 978-1-9163024-3-3

First published in Great Britain in 2020 by GMI - Guitar & Music Institute

GMI - Guitar & Music Institute is the trading name of Guitar & Music Online Learning Ltd.

Cover design by Ged Brockie

TABLE OF CONTENTS

**Difficulty rating 1 = easy to 5 = harder

SONG	PAGE #	# PAGES	DIFFICULTY	ERA
All Along The Watchtower	10	2	5	60s
All The Small Things	12	3	2	90s
Barbara Ann	15	3	5	60s
Breakfast At Tiffany's	18	2	2	90s
Cecilia	20	2	1	70s
Chasing Cars	22	3	3	90s
Common People	25	3	3	90s
Give Me One Reason	28	2	3	90s
Happier	30	2	2	10s
High And Dry	32	2	1	90s
I Gotta Feeling	34	2	2	00s
I Have A Dream	36	5	5	70s
I Still Haven't Found What I'm Looking For	41	3	4	80s
Just The Way You Are	44	2	2	10s
Leaving On A Jet Plane	46	2	1	60s
Little Ghost	48	2	1	90s
Mustang Sally	50	2	2	60s
Red Red Wine	52	3	2	80s
Royals	55	2	1	10s
Seven Bridges Roads	57	3	1	80s
Shake It Off	60	2	2	10s
Sweet Home Alabama	62	2	3	70s
The First Cut Is The Deepest	64	5	1	00s
The Tide Is High	69	2	4	80s
The Joker	71	2	3	70s
Walk Of Life	73	3	2	80s
Walk On The Wild Side	76	2	2	70s

TABLE OF CONTENTS - Difficulty rating 1 = easy to 5 = harder

HOW WE DECIDED ON A SONG'S DIFFICULTY RATING

You may find some songs in this book not that difficult to play re the chords but they're rated harder to play than other songs which at first glance may seem more complex. In arriving at a difficulty rating, we not only looked at the chords, for example open chords versus barre chords but also suggested rhythms, song form in general and down and up stokes in the rhythm.

In some songs there are complex openings or endings etc. All of these factors are added together when deciding on the complexity and the relative difficulty of a song, not just the chords themselves.

If you don't bother with the suggested rhythms provided, the vast majority of songs will be of a complexity that most beginners to advancing guitarists will easily get under their fingers in a reasonably short time. If you do persevere with the suggested rhythms and remember, they are just "suggested rhythms", then you'll have a sound that is much closer to the original recording that you are playing along with.

APPENDICES

GETTING THE MOST FROM THIS SONGBOOK

This book includes some of the biggest hits from a wide timeframe of popular music that you could ever wish to play on guitar. All songs can be played with just three chords per song. Make sure you read this guide to get off to a flying start and get the most from this book.

USING THE QR CODES…WHAT'S A QR CODE READER?

If you are not familiar with what a QR code is, it's the box shown on every page with funny marks on it shown just under the WATCH - LISTEN - PLAY ALONG heading.

Using a search engine of your choice, type in "free QR code reader", there are many to choose from. Select one and download it to your cell/mobile phone or tablet. Once installed, open the app up and point it at one of the squares, keeping your hand steady. It will recognise the web address in the box and notify you once it has worked it's magic.

It will offer to open up the video that has been added to the QR box you are pointing at. You can watch and listen to the song or use the opened video to play along with the song as you learn it.

THREE CHORDS ARE SHOWN, HOW DOES IT WORK?

All songs listed in this book have three chords per song. Many online resources say that such and such a song has three chords, but in this publication, you can be confident that the song does actually only contain three chords and is not a cut down version of song which has a lot more chords in it. In a couple of examples we have included alternate chords as well as inverted chords (chords that have the same notes but start on different notes within the chord).

WHAT IS PROVIDED FOR EACH SONG?

We have included both chords for each song, handy notes on how best to play the song as well as a top tips box. The chords are shown in large format as well as within the "Suggested Rhythm" page of the book.

WHAT IS A SUGGESTED RHYTHM?

The suggested rhythm is just that; a rhythmic idea we feel best reflects the rhythm and melody of the song you are learning. We have added some resources to help you understand how to read rhythms.

On the following pages we have included rhythm exercises and explanations for you to practice before diving in to the songs proper.

We have also added a "rhythm tree" at the back of the book in the appendices for you to study if you are interested in understanding more about rhythm.

ARE THERE ANY OTHER WAYS IN WHICH THIS BOOK HELP ME WITH GUITAR?

Yes. We have also included four pages of common open string chords that can be found at the bottom of the guitar neck which are often described as "open string chords". **Download the free practice & demo rhythm tracks! You can find out how on page 101**

ALL THE BEST WITH YOUR GUITAR PLAYING FROM

GMI - GUITAR & MUSIC INSTITUTE

VISIT OUR WEBSITE FOR FREE HD GUITAR LESSONS, PODCASTS, ARTICLES AND RESOURCES

www.guitarandmusicinstitute.com

VISIT OUR ONLINE SHOP FOR FREE & PAID RESOURCES THAT WILL TAKE YOUR GUITAR TO THE NEXT LEVEL

https://gmiguitarshop.com

LEARNING TO PLAY THE SUGGESTED RHYTHMS

Each song presented in this book includes a suggested rhythm. If you have never read music or rhythms before, the pages that follow will help you understand how to interpret the examples given.

DOWN & UP STROKES

These symbols are seen above each rhythm presented and tell you to either strum a chord with a down stroke ⊓ (hold the pick and strum the strings down to the floor) or an upstroke ∨ which is away from the floor upwards towards the upper part of the guitar body.

EXAMPLES FOR UNDERSTANDING RHYTHMIC NOTATION

Count to four. If you can do this, then you can read these rhythms! Always give yourself a count of four before you start playing the rhythm. In the first example, choose a chord, count to four then strum when you say "one" the second time round. A diamond with no stem is worth four beats.

Example #1

Example #2

In this next example, we still play down strokes, but the rhythm is played every two beats. Remember, a diamond headed note with a stem is worth two beats. Choose a chord to play, give yourself a count in of four then play the following rhythm.

Example #3

The third example has you playing four down strokes in each bar. As usual, choose a chord to play give yourself a count of four then strum four times in each bar. A slash with a stem is worth one beat.

Example #4

In this fourth example you can see a couple of other symbols. The percentage sign symbol in the second bar simply means you repeat what you have played in the previous bar. If you look under the rhythm symbol on beats two and four you will see a dot. This dot means cut the beat short.

Example #5

This example shows a very common rhythm used in popular music. You not only play down on your chord but up strokes as well. You are now playing two strums per beat. This is shown by the fact that all the slash rhythm notes are joined together and you count 1 & 2 & etc.

Example #6

Okay, things are getting a little more complex now. What you are viewing in example number six is the following: the first bar has "eighth" notes as in the previous example, but it has a "tie" between the & of 2 and 3.

You play an upstroke on the & of 2 then DO NOT hit the strings on the down stroke on beat 3; play a "ghost" stroke and let the chord keep ringing through 3 as you play. Hit an upstroke on the & of 3 as you proceed. In the second bar you will see that a tie leads into the bar and then the funny little "7" symbols are called rests.

Play ghost strokes on these counts. A ghost stroke is where you make the movement with your arm but you do not make contact with the strings. Damping the string vibration with your left hand (assuming your right handed) so that no sound is heard on these beats.

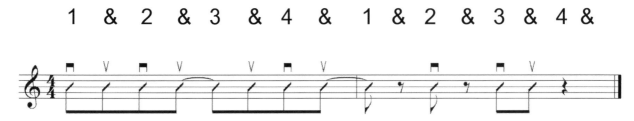

Example #7

In quite a few of the songs presented there is a funky beat. One of the hallmarks of funk music is the fast rhythms used. Here you can see them and they are called sixteenth rhythms. There are four movements of the arm to every beat - down up down up. Play this slowly to get used to it.

Example #8

This final example is without doubt complex and will take some time for you to understand and play. It includes sixteenth rhythms with sixteenth rests and ties. This is a good example of a musical term called "syncopation" which is used in funk music on a regular basis. For more help in understanding rhythms, check out the "rhythm tree" provided in the appendices at the end of this book.

SONGS

All Along The Watchtower

- **Artist: Bob Dylan (Jimi Hendrix version)**
- **Released: 1968**

NOTES: Although initially written and released by Bob Dylan, the version that most people think of and is synonymous with the nineteen sixties is the Jimi Hendrix version. The Jimi version of Bob's song was again brought to prominence in the 1980's with the release of the (over time) cult film "Withnail and I" and the memorable police chase car scene.

Although Jimi plays riffs and solos on the song, again it's surprising to learn that the whole song can be played with just three chords. When playing the intro it's important to count, so have a look at the opening pages of this publication to help you count and play together.

WATCH - LISTEN - PLAY ALONG!

THE 3 CHORDS USED

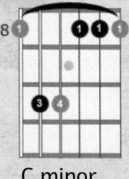

C minor

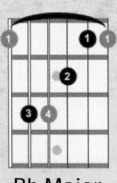

Bb Major

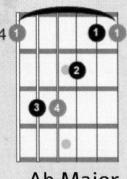

Ab Major

TOP TIP: Barre chords (which all these three chords are) can be difficult for those who have never tried them before.

Try not to press down with your first finger hard over all frets, but apply pressure (especially on the middle strings) with the middle part of your first finger that is making the barre.

For the C minor chord, try and put your second finger over the first finger barre to give it extra support.

CONTINUE OVERLEAF…

All Along The Watchtower

SUGGESTED CHORD RHYTHM & SONG STRUCTURE

WATCH - LISTEN - PLAY ALONG!

SONG STRUCTURE

Intro - verse - instrumental - verse - instrumental - verse - instrumental

INTRO & INSTRUMENTAL SECTIONS

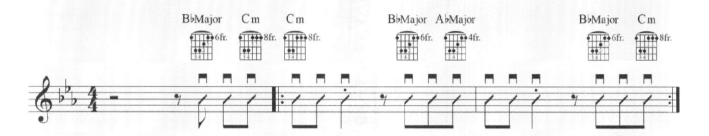

VERSE

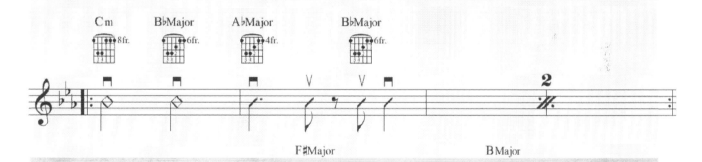

SONG STRUCTURE

Intro - verse - instrumental - verse - instrumental - verse - instrumental

All The Small Things

- **Artist: Blink – 182**
- **Released: 1999 and re released 2000**

NOTES: Blink – 182 had their biggest hit which broke into the top forty around the world with this song which was backed up with a very much tongue in cheek video which by all accounts continues to be extremely popular with over two hundred and fifty million views on Youtube.

With over a million sales in the UK which was double the sales in America, All The Small Things received many accolades including Rolling Stone placing it in 94th place in it's top one hundred greatest ever pop songs...not bad for the bands only big hit.

WATCH - LISTEN - PLAY ALONG!

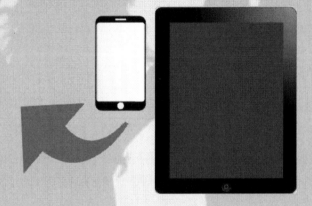

THE 3 CHORDS USED

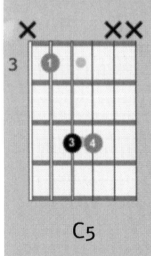

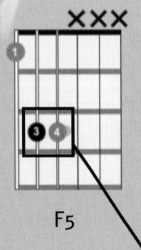

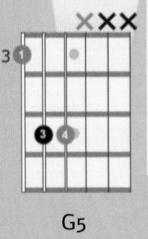

C5   F5   G5

TOP TIPS: Although there are only three chords used in this song (power chords for a heavier rock sound) there is a fourth shape offered overleaf. This is an inversion of one of the chords played. Same chord, same notes but in a different order.

NOTE: Just play these two notes to play F5/C

CONTINUE OVERLEAF...

All The Small Things

SUGGESTED CHORD RHYTHM & SONG STRUCTURE

WATCH - LISTEN - PLAY ALONG!

SONG STRUCTURE

Intro/interlude - verse - pre chorus - chorus - verse - pre chorus

- chorus - interlude 2 - chorus

INTRO/INTERLUDE

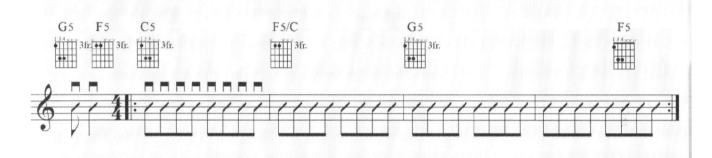

VERSE

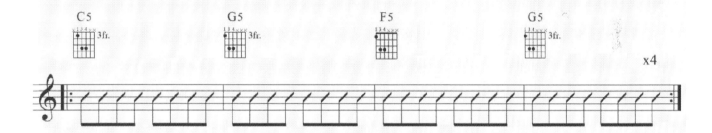

PRE CHORUS

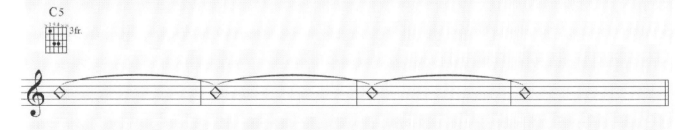

CONTINUE OVERLEAF...

All The Small Things

SUGGESTED CHORD RHYTHM & SONG STRUCTURE

WATCH - LISTEN - PLAY ALONG!

SONG STRUCTURE

Intro/interlude - verse - pre chorus - chorus - verse - pre chorus
- chorus - interlude 2 - chorus

CHORUS

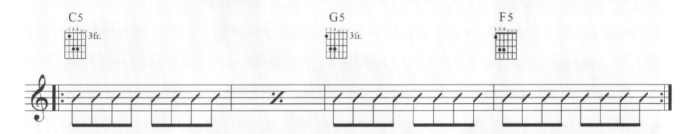

INTRO/INTERLUDE

VERSE (two times only)

PRE CHORUS

CHORUS

INTERLUDE 2 (below)

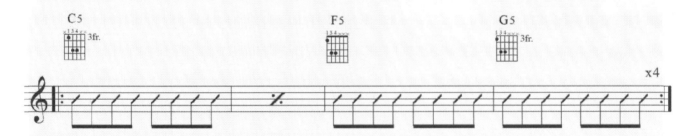

CHORUS TILL END

SONG STRUCTURE

Intro/interlude - verse - - pre chorus - chorus - verse - pre chorus
- chorus - interlude 2 - chorus

Barbara Ann

- Artist: Beachboys
- Released: 1965

NOTES: Fred Fassert composed Barbara Ann and several years later was initially recorded and released by a band named "The Regents" in 1961. It was the Beachboys, however, that created the hit that most people will immediately think of.

This is another song that you will need to work hard to achieve if you have not already got your barre chords together. As well as this, there is a tricky change to the C#7 chord which will take some time for most to manage.

WATCH - LISTEN - PLAY ALONG!

THE 3 CHORDS USED

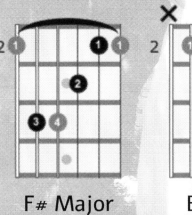

F# Major   B Major   C#7

TOP TIP: The song Barbara Ann is loosely based around the blues progression and as such, it's a great song to learn because thousands of other songs use a similar sequence of chords (usually in other key centres).

To play this song you need to NOT PLAY at times! Listen to the track via the QR code above and notice how many times the instruments are NOT playing. Learning when not to play will add excitement when you do re-enter.

CONTINUE OVERLEAF...

Barbara Ann

SUGGESTED CHORD RHYTHM & SONG STRUCTURE

WATCH - LISTEN - PLAY ALONG!

SONG STRUCTURE

A - B - A - C (instrumental) - B - A - D (section D is the same as section A but with no intro two bars of vocals only at beginning)

SECTIONS (SEE OVERLEAF FOR SONG STRUCTURE)

CONTINUE OVERLEAF...

Barbara Ann

SUGGESTED CHORD RHYTHM & SONG STRUCTURE

WATCH - LISTEN - PLAY ALONG!

SONG STRUCTURE

A - B - A - C (instrumental) - B - A - D (section D is the same as section A but with no intro two bars of vocals only at beginning)

SECTIONS Cont...

SONG STRUCTURE

A - B - A - C (instrumental) - B - A - D (section D is the same as section A but with no intro two bars of vocals only at beginning)

Breakfast At Tiffany's

- **Artist: Deep Blue Something**
- **Released: 1995**

NOTES: Yet another song that was the band in question's only big hit. This song charted around the world hitting the number one spot in the UK and Scottish charts. It also reached top ten status in nine other countries/territories and charted top ten in four out of six mainstream American charts so...not bad!

You can watch and play along with the official video which has forty million views and must be a bit of an cash cow in its own right. The film Roman Holiday was the inspiration for the song, but any chance to include Audrey Hepburn in proceedings couldn't be missed hence the title.

WATCH - LISTEN - PLAY ALONG!

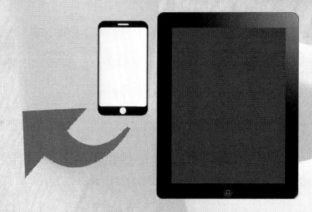

THE 3 CHORDS USED

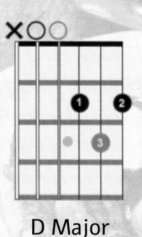

D Major

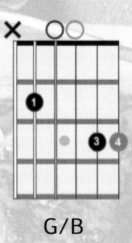

G/B

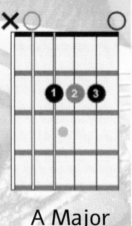

A Major

TOP TIPS: This song includes another example of a major chord which has a note that is not the root note (name of chord) in the bass.

The G major chord has a "B" note in the bass. This note is the 3rd of the G Major scale and when the 3rd is in the bass it's called a first inversion.

CONTINUE OVERLEAF...

Breakfast At Tiffany's

SUGGESTED CHORD RHYTHM & SONG STRUCTURE

WATCH - LISTEN - PLAY ALONG!

SONG STRUCTURE

Intro - verse - chorus - gtr. Interlude - verse - chorus - verse - chorus - gtr. Interlude - chorus till end

Verse

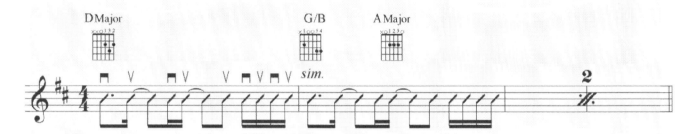

Chorus

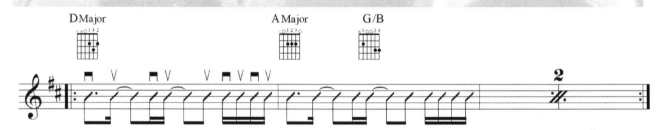

SONG STRUCTURE

The entire song is constructed out of the four bars shown above. The various parts of the song play the four bars a certain number of times.

Introduction x 1, Verse x 4, Chorus x 2

Guitar Interlude x 1

Verse x 4, Chorus x 2, Verse x 4, Chorus x 2

Guitar Interlude x 2

Chorus x 4

Cecilia

- **Artist: Simon & Garfunkel**
- **Released: 1970**

NOTES: Paul Simon wrote this song at a party and it's named after the patron saint of music who is Saint Cecilia, but in the song he refers to her as an untrustworthy lover.

The song was a hit in numerous countries charting number one in the USA "cash box" and Netherlands chart lists.

Very much a song to sing at get together's and party occasions, it makes sense when you think where the song was first composed.

WATCH - LISTEN - PLAY ALONG!

THE 3 CHORDS USED

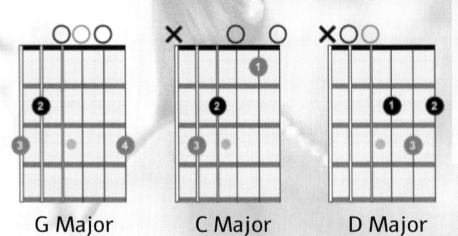

G Major   C Major   D Major

TOP TIPS: Although as always, the chords are important, what makes this song is a robust right hand rhythmic pattern.

Make sure you give it plenty of welly with a louder the better approach!

CONTINUE OVERLEAF...

Cecilia

SUGGESTED CHORD RHYTHM & SONG STRUCTURE

WATCH - LISTEN - PLAY ALONG!

SONG STRUCTURE

Intro - verse - verse - chorus - verse - chorus - drum solo -
refrain till end

INTRO, VERSE & DRUM SOLO SECTION

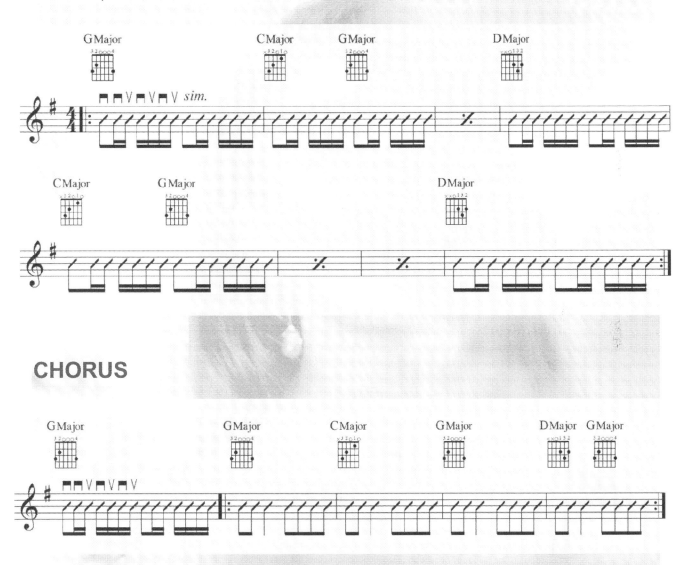

CHORUS

SONG STRUCTURE

Intro - verse - verse - chorus - verse - chorus - drum solo -
refrain till end

21

Chasing Cars

- Artist: Snow Patrol
- Released: 2006

NOTES: A Northern Irish/Scottish group that has seen this song from their fourth album "Eyes Open" amass over 230,000,000 views on Youtube; yes, read that number again...

The song has only three chords that are shown below with a repetitive and hypnotic melody played over the top. This publications shows you how to play the chords as shown below.

As of 2020 the band continue to record and tour with this song being voted in one pole as the song most played at funerals!

WATCH - LISTEN - PLAY ALONG!

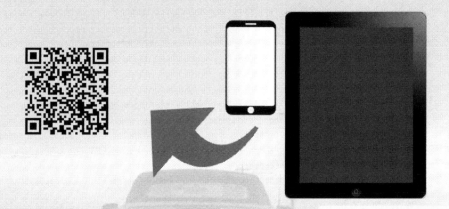

THE 3 CHORDS USED

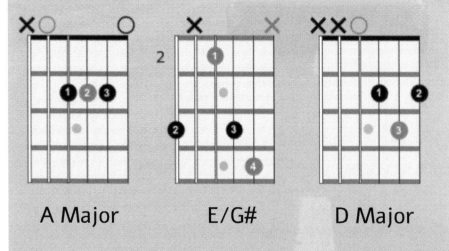

A Major   E/G#   D Major

TOP TIP: The second chord E major with a G sharp in the bass will be quite tricky for most players to begin with.

To make things a little easier, you should know that this is a D Major chord (as in the third chord) taken up two frets.

The first finger takes the place of the open string and the second finger in playing the bass note is the same note that the second finger is playing on string one open D chord.

CONTINUE OVERLEAF...

Chasing Cars

SUGGESTED CHORD RHYTHM & SONG STRUCTURE

WATCH - LISTEN - PLAY ALONG!

SONG STRUCTURE

verse - chorus - verse - chorus - verse - chorus - chorus

- bridge - chorus

VERSE

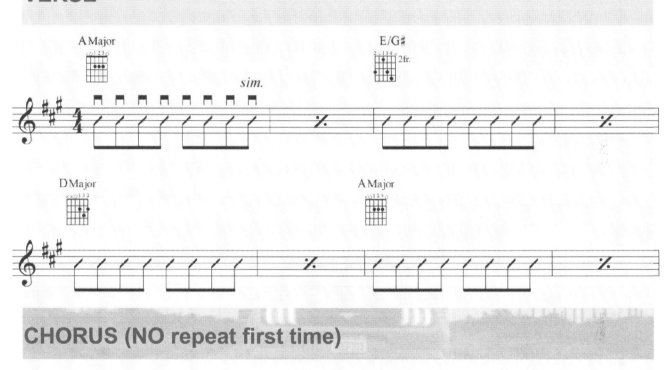

CHORUS (NO repeat first time)

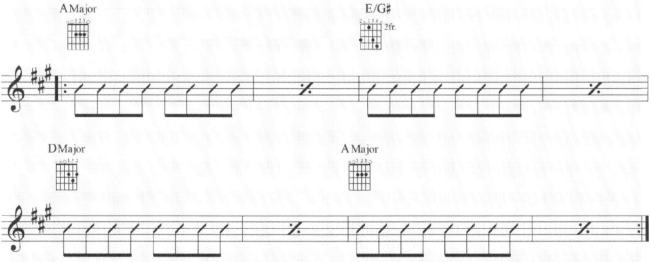

CONTINUE OVERLEAF...

Chasing Cars

SUGGESTED CHORD RHYTHM & SONG STRUCTURE

WATCH - LISTEN - PLAY ALONG!

SONG STRUCTURE

verse - chorus - verse - chorus - verse - chorus - chorus - bridge - chorus

BRIDGE

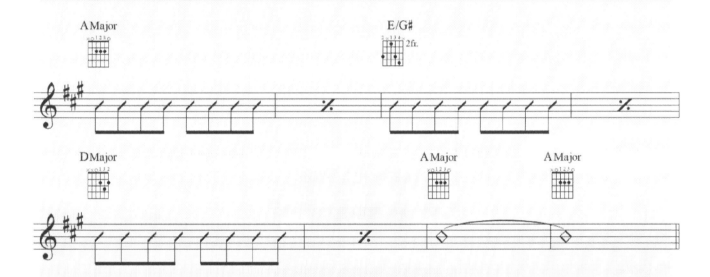

SONG STRUCTURE

verse - chorus - verse - chorus - verse - chorus - chorus - bridge - chorus

Common People

- **Artist: Pulp**
- **Released: 1995**

NOTES: This song reached number two in the UK charts and became the song most associated with the Britpop movement in the UK during the 90s.

Covered over the years by many people, it's even had a version released by William Shatner aka "Captain Kirk" of Star Trek fame!

The suggested rhythm on the next page could just as easily shown constant up and down strokes (eighths). Look to increase the volume of your rhythm as the song continues.

WATCH - LISTEN - PLAY ALONG!

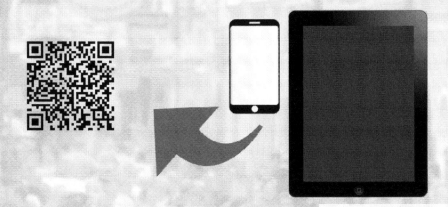

THE 3 CHORDS USED

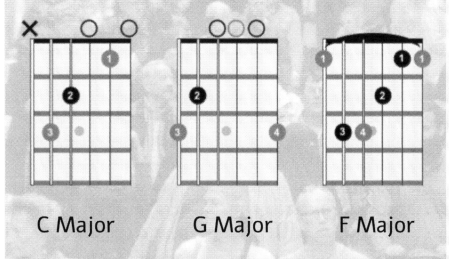

C Major   G Major   F Major

TOP TIP: There is a tricky introduction to barre chords in the form of the F Major chord which is chord three to the left of this box.

There is an "open" version of the F Major chord, but by mastering this version, you will be able to take chords all the way up the neck and rename.

This will mean you will be able to play every major chord including sharp and flat chords with this one shape.

CONTINUE OVERLEAF...

Common People

SUGGESTED CHORD RHYTHM & SONG STRUCTURE

WATCH - LISTEN - PLAY ALONG!

SONG STRUCTURE

Intro - verse - chorus - verse - chorus - bridge - chorus -
instrumental - chorus - verse - bridge - chorus

INTRO & VERSE (note bridge is the same as verse)

CONTINUE OVERLEAF…

Common People

SUGGESTED CHORD RHYTHM & SONG STRUCTURE

WATCH - LISTEN - PLAY ALONG!

SONG STRUCTURE

Intro - verse - chorus - verse - chorus - bridge - chorus -
instrumental - chorus - verse - bridge - chorus

CHORUS & SOLO SECTION

SONG STRUCTURE

Intro - verse - chorus - verse - chorus - bridge - chorus -
instrumental - chorus - verse - bridge - chorus

Give Me One Reason

- ●Artist: Tracy Chapman
- ●Released: 1995

NOTES: With all the amazing songs that she's written to date, we were slightly surprised that this blues based song has actually been Tracy's biggest hit so far which just goes to show us and everyone else the enduring power and popularity of the blues. Hitting number one in the US adult top 40 as well as number one in Canada and Iceland, this track sold over a million copies in the USA alone.

At nearly fifteen million views on Youtube, Give Me One Reason shows no sign of loosing it's appeal anytime soon.

WATCH - LISTEN - PLAY ALONG!

THE 3 CHORDS USED

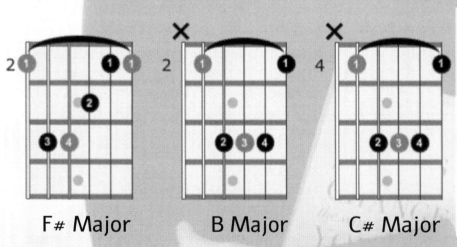

F# Major   B Major   C# Major

TOP TIPS: This is one of those songs that if you can play barre chords it's a total breeze, if you can't; it's a total nightmare.

If you can't play barre chords, sometimes it feels like they will never come, however, keep working at it and you will eventually crack them.

CONTINUE OVERLEAF...

Give Me One Reason

SUGGESTED CHORD RHYTHM & SONG STRUCTURE

WATCH - LISTEN - PLAY ALONG!

SONG STRUCTURE

Intro - verse - chorus - verse - chorus - solo section - chorus till end

INTRO

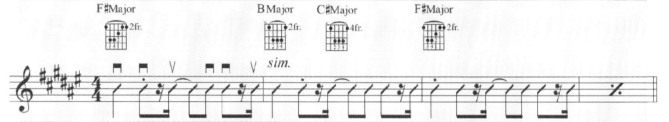

VERSE & CHORUS

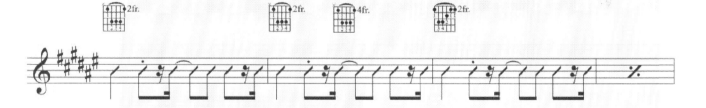

SONG STRUCTURE

Intro - verse - chorus - verse - chorus - solo section - chorus till end

Happier

- Artist: Ed Sheeran
- Released: 2018

NOTES: A song that was released on Ed's third album. Apparently the song refers to a time in his life when a girl he was once with ended up with someone else and he's happy that she's happy. The song has charted across the world and made number six in the UK singles chart.

The same three chords are played the same way for the majority of the song. The only difference being that the rhythm in the chorus can be a little more strident than the finger style accompaniment which is used in the verse.

WATCH - LISTEN - PLAY ALONG!

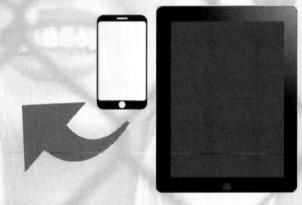

THE 3 CHORDS USED

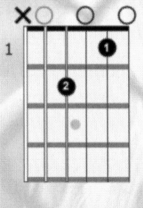

A minor 7

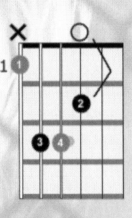

F Major

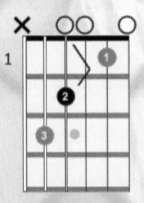

C Major

TOP TIPS: You will see the crooked lines on the chord boxes for F Major and C Major.

These refer to "hammer on" options when playing these two chords. To play a "hammer on" you play the chord with the open option then quickly bring down your second finger like a piano hammer (look it up on Youtube) or even "strike like a Python!").

A great sound to add to this song as played by Ed.

CONTINUE OVERLEAF…

Happier

SUGGESTED CHORD RHYTHM & SONG STRUCTURE

WATCH - LISTEN - PLAY ALONG!

SONG STRUCTURE

Intro - verse - pre chorus - chorus - verse - pre chorus - chorus -
refrain till end

VERSE & PRE CHORUS & CHORUS

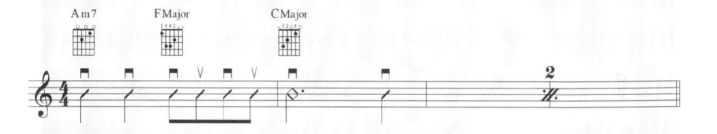

SONG STRUCTURE

Intro - verse - pre chorus - chorus - verse - pre chorus -
chorus - refrain till end

High And Dry

- Artist: Radiohead
- Released: 1995

NOTES: Not one of Radiohead's biggest hits, but without doubt a firm favorite with their fans and certainly a song that can easily be identified amongst the many songs that the band have produced.

With over forty million views on Youtube at the time of this publication, the song has done better when packaged with the video as it never really hit the highest heights. The song reached eleventh in Canada, eleventh in Iceland, seventeen in the UK singles chart and position twenty one in the Scottish chart which was the highest top four rankings.

WATCH - LISTEN - PLAY ALONG!

THE 3 CHORDS USED

TOP TIPS: You will see on the following page that the suggested rhythm is to play a heavy down stroke on beats two and four and to cut the beat short to give a percussive quality to the sound.

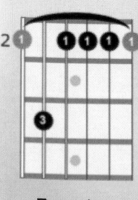

F# minor 7

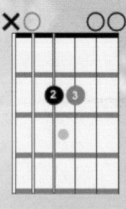

A sus2

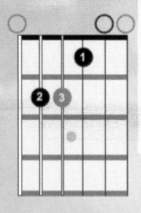

E Major

CONTINUE OVERLEAF...

High And Dry

SUGGESTED CHORD RHYTHM & SONG STRUCTURE

WATCH - LISTEN - PLAY ALONG!

SONG STRUCTURE

Intro - verse - chorus - guitar break - verse - chorus - gtr. solo - vocal interlude - chorus till end

INTRO, VERSE, CHORUS

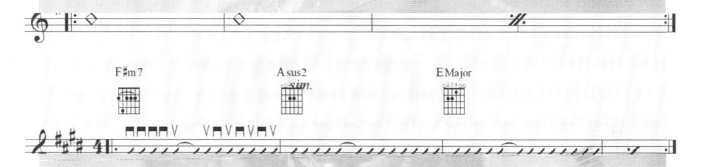

F#m7   A sus2   E Major

SONG STRUCTURE

The entire song is constructed out of the four bars shown above. The various parts of the song play the four bars a certain number of times.

Introduction (after drums) x 2

Verse x 4

Chorus x 2

Guitar break x 1

Verse x 4

Chorus x 2

Guitar solo x 2

Vocal Interlude x 2

Chorus x 4

I Gotta Feeling

- Artist: The Black Eyed Peas
- Released: 2009

NOTES: Quite a song ranking fifth in the Billboard top 100 songs of the decade I Gotta Feeling was from the Black Eyed Peas fifth album hitting the heights in a slew of countries around the world.

This song is included as we there are not that many dance related songs in this book. The song really just does the same thing again and again, you probably won't find it the most engaging of all the chords and sequences found here. With nearly five hundred million views on Youtube which shows it's popularity it had to be included!

WATCH - LISTEN - PLAY ALONG!

THE 3 MAIN CHORDS USED

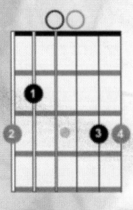
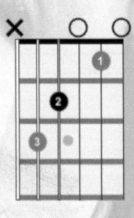
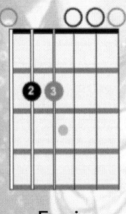

G Major   C Major   E minor

TOP TIPS: You will definitely find these chords a challenge.

Keep working at it because when you do get these chords together they open up a new range of song possibilities. Play a simple picking pattern on these chords for best effect.

CONTINUE OVERLEAF...

I Gotta Feeling

SUGGESTED CHORD RHYTHM & SONG STRUCTURE

SONG STRUCTURE

Intro - verse - chorus - verse - pre chorus - chorus

WATCH - LISTEN - PLAY ALONG!

INTRO - VERSE - PRE CHORUS - CHORUS

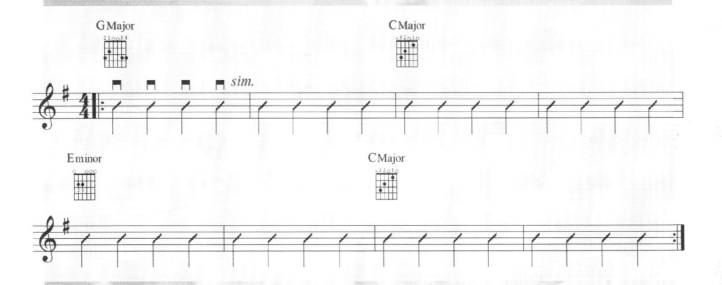

SONG STRUCTURE

Intro - verse - chorus - verse - pre chorus - chorus

I Have A Dream

- Artist: Abba
- Released: 1979

NOTES: A song that is the soundtrack to a generation, well almost! Abba's "I Have A Dream" topped the charts around the world but it stopped at position number two in the UK by "Another Brick In The Wall" by Pink Floyd.

Although only three chords this song is a challenge! One of the biggest hurdles to get over is that the number of beats in each bar (within the intro specifically but not exclusively) changes quite a bit. Make sure you count really hard and follow the suggested rhythms as shown over the next few pages.

WATCH - LISTEN - PLAY ALONG!

THE 3 CHORDS USED

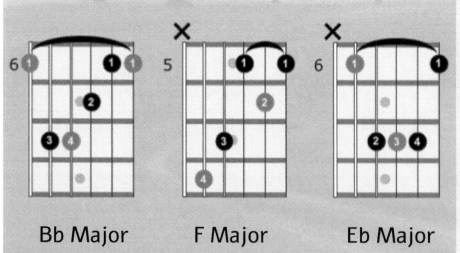

Bb Major   F Major   Eb Major

TOP TIPS: Work on the barre chords first before attempting the song as trying to get both together at the same time is a big ask.

Make sure you read the ENGLISH in the following pages which tells you where you need to go next in the song.

The song has lots of little changes which has meant that we have had to spread it over four pages so read carefully.

CONTINUE OVERLEAF...

I Have A Dream

SUGGESTED CHORD RHYTHM & SONG STRUCTURE

WATCH - LISTEN - PLAY ALONG!

SONG STRUCTURE

Intro - verse & chorus 1 - verse & chorus 2 - instrumental
- verse & chorus 3 - instrumental ending

INTRO

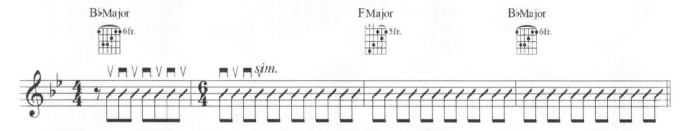

VERSE & CHORUS 1

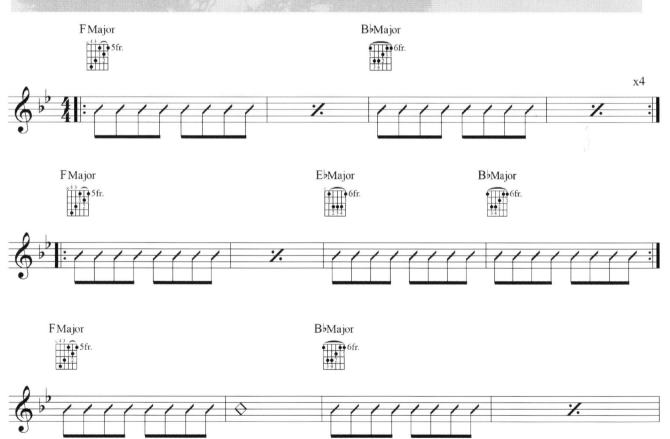

CONTINUE OVERLEAF...

I Have A Dream

SUGGESTED CHORD RHYTHM & SONG STRUCTURE

WATCH - LISTEN - PLAY ALONG!

SONG STRUCTURE

Intro - verse & chorus 1 - verse & chorus 2 - instrumental
- verse & chorus 3 - instrumental ending

VERSE & CHORUS 2 & 3

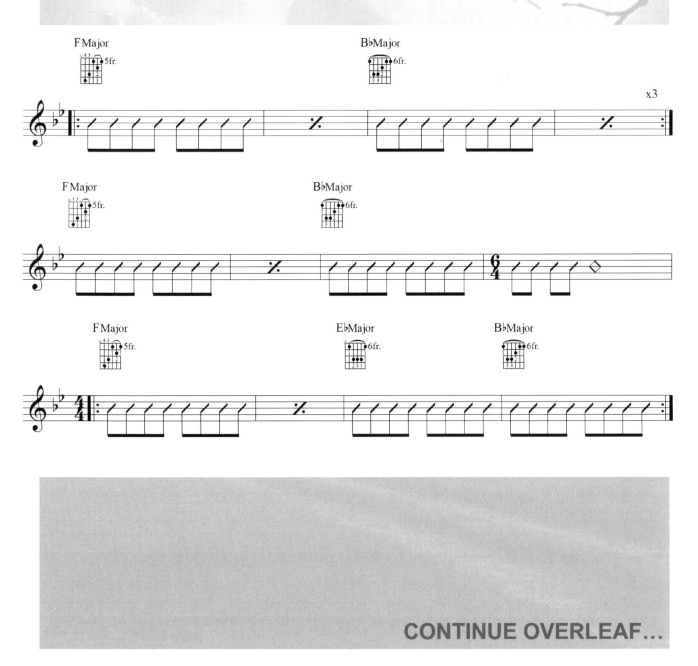

CONTINUE OVERLEAF…

I Have A Dream

SUGGESTED CHORD RHYTHM & SONG STRUCTURE

WATCH - LISTEN - PLAY ALONG!

SONG STRUCTURE

Intro - verse & chorus 1 - verse & chorus 2 - instrumental
- verse & chorus 3 - instrumental ending

VERSE & CHORUS 2 & 3 Cont...

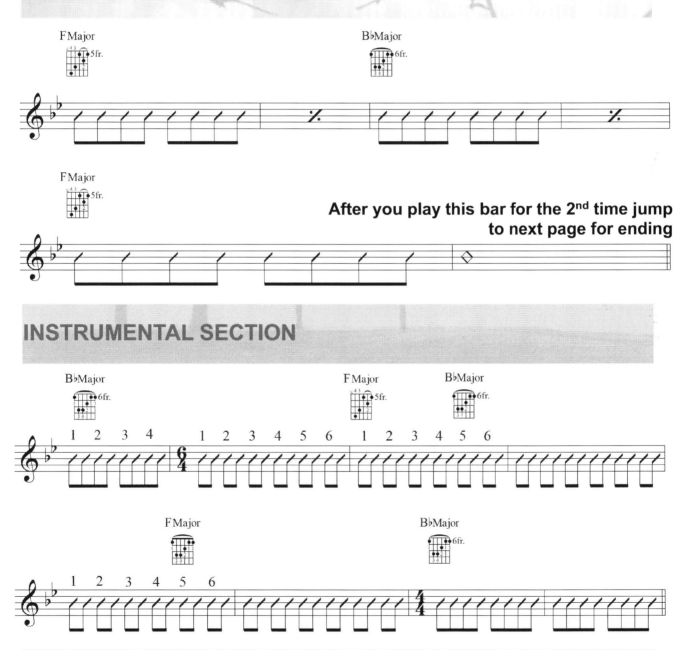

After you play this bar for the 2nd time jump
to next page for ending

INSTRUMENTAL SECTION

NOW GO BACK ONE PAGE AND PLAY 3rd VERSE & CHORUS

I Have A Dream

SUGGESTED CHORD RHYTHM & SONG STRUCTURE

WATCH - LISTEN - PLAY ALONG!

SONG STRUCTURE

Intro - verse & chorus 1 - verse & chorus 2 - instrumental
- verse & chorus 3 - instrumental ending

INSTRUMENTAL ENDING

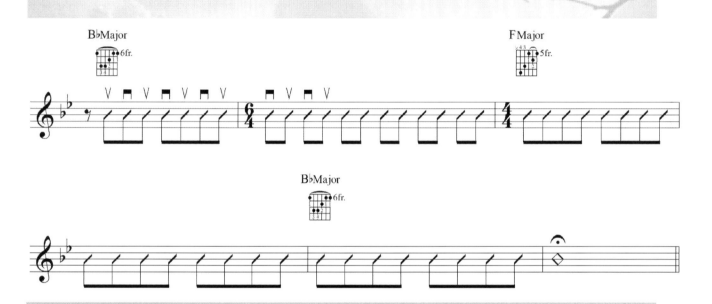

SONG STRUCTURE

Intro - verse & chorus 1 - verse & chorus 2 - instrumental - verse & chorus 3 - instrumental ending

I Still Haven't Found What I'm Looking For

- Artist: U2
- Released: 1987

NOTES: As this song has without doubt, the longest name of any song featured in this book we have had to keep the notes on it down to a minimum. This was U2's second consecutive number one hit as it reached the US Billboard Top 100 at number one and the rest, as they say, is history. These are the bare chords for the tune as it's a bit much to expect you to run out and spend thousands on a guitar rig so you can sound like "The Edge" from U2.

WATCH - LISTEN - PLAY ALONG!

THE 3 MAIN CHORDS USED

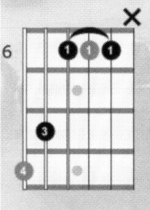

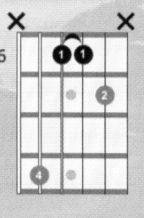

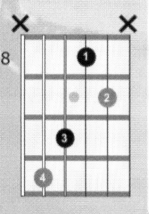

C# Major   F# sus2   G# Major

TOP TIPS: Although you may as mentioned at the top of this page not be willing to part with loads of money to get the U2 guitar sound, a much cheaper option is not to strum the chords, but to pick out notes from the chords. This is how you arpeggiate a chord; play individual notes from it.

CONTINUE OVERLEAF...

I Still Haven't Found What I'm Looking For

SUGGESTED CHORD RHYTHM & SONG STRUCTURE

WATCH - LISTEN - PLAY ALONG!

SONG STRUCTURE

Intro - verse - chorus - verse - chorus - gtr. Interlude - chorus till end of song

(INTRO FIRST FOUR BARS THEN VERSE BEGINS AT TOP)

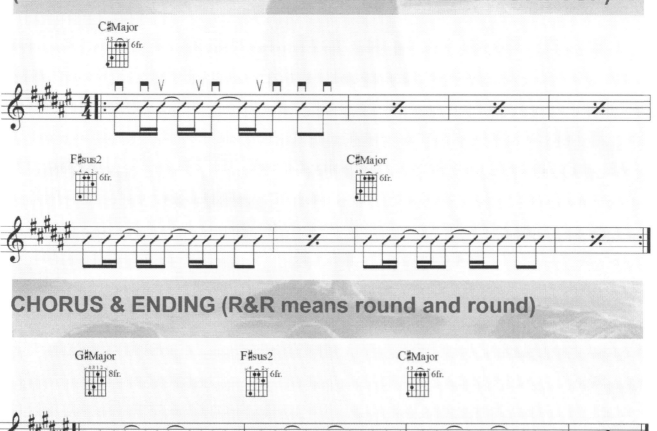

CHORUS & ENDING (R&R means round and round)

CONTINUE OVERLEAF…

I Still Haven't Found What I'm Looking For

SUGGESTED CHORD RHYTHM & SONG STRUCTURE

WATCH - LISTEN - PLAY ALONG!

SONG STRUCTURE

Intro - verse - chorus - verse - chorus - gtr. Interlude - chorus till end of song

GUITAR INTERLUDE

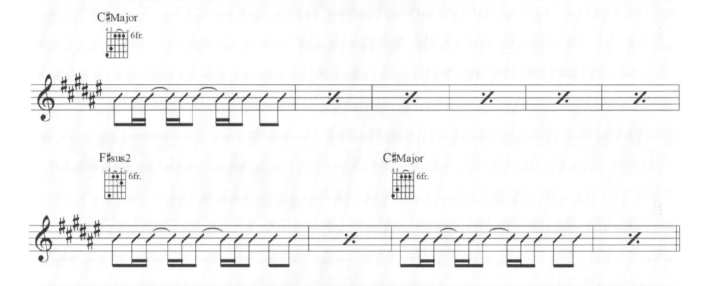

SONG STRUCTURE

Intro - verse - chorus - verse - chorus - gtr. Interlude - chorus till end of song

43

Just The Way You Are

- Artist: Bruno Mars
- Released: 2010

NOTES: Written by Bruno Mars and four other fellow musicians who are collectively called the "Smeezingtons", this was the the debut solo single from the debut solo album by Bruno Mars.

The song, as you'd expect from a book based on songs that have three chords has, well three chords but apparently Bruno said that it took months to write this song. It can only be assumed that he was talking about the lyrics.

Although thought of as a little on the gushy side by some, it didn't stop this song becoming a smash hit around the world!

WATCH - LISTEN - PLAY ALONG!

THE 3 CHORDS USED

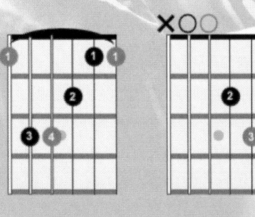

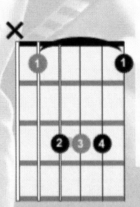

F Major   D minor   Bb Major

TOP TIPS: You will see on the following page that the suggested rhythm is to play a heavy down stroke on beats two and four and to cut the beat short to give a percussive quality to the sound.

CONTINUE OVERLEAF...

Just The Way You Are

SUGGESTED CHORD RHYTHM & SONG STRUCTURE

WATCH - LISTEN - PLAY ALONG!

SONG STRUCTURE

Intro - verse - chorus - verse - chorus - interlude - chorus

INTRO, VERSE, CHORUS & INTERLUDE

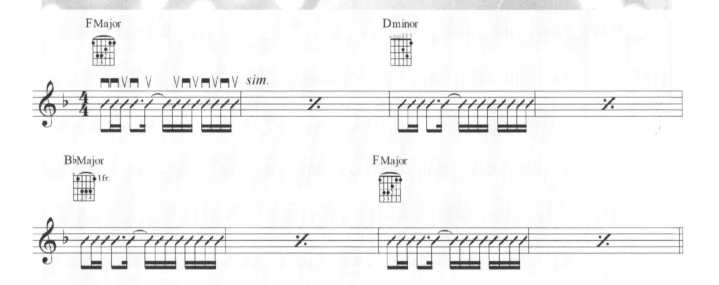

SONG STRUCTURE
Intro - verse - chorus - verse - chorus - interlude - chorus

Leaving On A Jet Plane

- Artist: John Denver
- Released: 1969

NOTES: John Denver composed around 200 hit songs, released 300 songs and sold over 33 million songs world wide! Huge in the nineteen seventies and eighties, John sadly died aged only 53 in a light plane accident in 1997.

A relatively easy rhythm that is made up of down and up strokes (eighth rhythm) will give you the sound you are looking for. This song can have other chords added, however, the three main chords are more than adequate to give you the true spirit of this well loved classic.

WATCH - LISTEN - PLAY ALONG!

THE 3 CHORDS USED

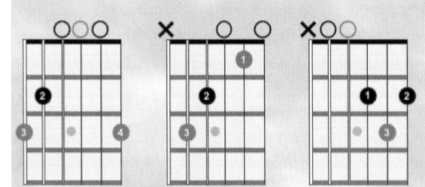

G Major   C Major   D Major

TOP TIP: This song is fairly quick and you should concentrate on keeping the "tempo" of your rhythm really tight (in time).

CONTINUE OVERLEAF…

Leaving On A Jet Plane

SUGGESTED CHORD RHYTHM & SONG STRUCTURE

WATCH - LISTEN - PLAY ALONG!

SONG STRUCTURE

verse - pre chorus - chorus - verse - pre chorus chorus -
verse - pre chorus - chorus

VERSE & PRE CHORUS

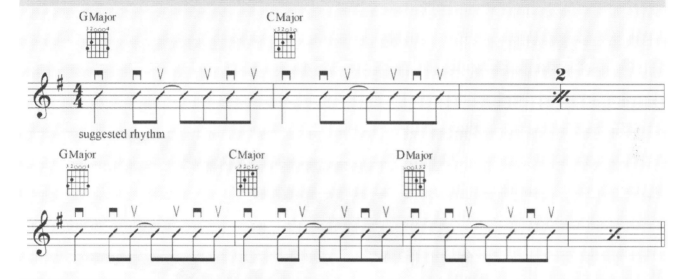

CHORUS

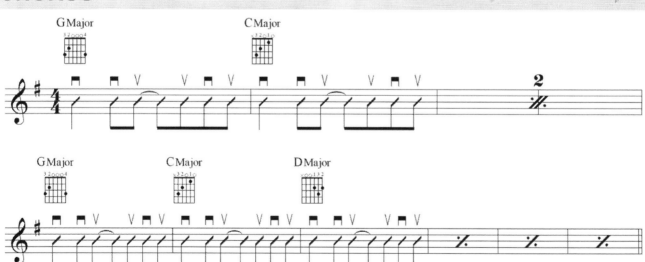

SONG STRUCTURE

verse - pre chorus - chorus x3

Little Ghost

- ●Artist: The White Stripes
- ●Released: 1995

NOTES: Little Ghost is a song from the White Stripes album "Get Behind Me Satan". If you've never read up on the creation of the album and the fact that it is a metaphor for the Hollywood superstar Rita Hayworth, then it's well worth a read.

A simple song and a more basic way of recording this album re guitar sound nevertheless this album, although never reaching number one, peaked in the top ten and even top five in a basket of countries around the globe.

WATCH - LISTEN - PLAY ALONG!

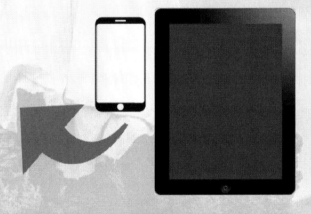

THE 3 CHORDS USED

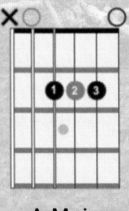

A Major

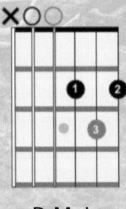

D Major

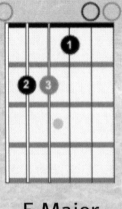

E Major

TOP TIPS: Little Ghost is all about the right hand rhythm playing (assuming your right handed that is) so take your time and work up the sound by using constant up and down strokes and missing out the hit on the strings whilst still making the action of your arm.

CONTINUE OVERLEAF…

Little Ghost

SUGGESTED CHORD RHYTHM & SONG STRUCTURE

WATCH - LISTEN - PLAY ALONG!

SONG STRUCTURE

Intro - verse - chorus - verse - chorus etc.

INTRO

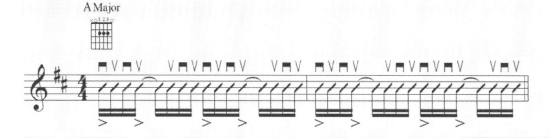

VERSE & CHORUS

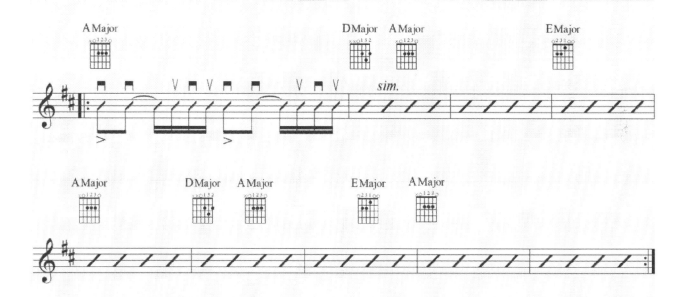

SONG STRUCTURE
The entire song is constructed out of the eight bars shown above both verse and chorus.

Mustang Sally

- Artist: Mack Rice
- Released: 1965

NOTES: First recorded and released by Mack Rice the song really took off the following year when Wilson Pickett released a cover of the single. The song got a new lease of life when in 1991 the film "The Commitments" was released to critical acclaim with this song featured heavily throughout.

Although not hard to play there are numerous ways that the the three chords could be played from R&B to heavy. The song form is twenty four bars long which is not that common compared to the usual thirty two bar form which was popular throughout the 20th century.

WATCH - LISTEN - PLAY ALONG!

THE 3 CHORDS USED

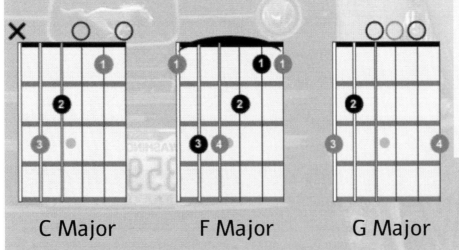

C Major   F Major   G Major

TOP TIPS: You will see on the following page that the suggested rhythm is to play a heavy down stroke on beats two and four and to cut the beat short to give a percussive quality to the sound.

CONTINUE OVERLEAF...

Mustang Sally

SUGGESTED CHORD RHYTHM & SONG STRUCTURE

WATCH - LISTEN - PLAY ALONG!

SONG STRUCTURE

Intro and all verse and chorus follow form below.

INTRO, VERSE, CHORUS

First line Intro x1 then repeat to start verse

C Major

F Major

C Major

G Major

F Major

C Major

SONG STRUCTURE

Intro and all verse and chorus follow form above

Red Red Wine

- Artist: Neil Diamond (UB40 version)
- Released: 1983

NOTES: When UB40 decided to cover Red Red Wine they had no idea that the original artist who composed the song was Neil Diamond, thinking that N. Diamond was a Jamaican musician...we all live and learn.

Despite being a cover song that has not stopped the popularity of the UB40 version racking up an impressive one hundred and thirty + million views on Youtube.

WATCH - LISTEN - PLAY ALONG!

THE 3 CHORDS USED

| Db Major | Gb Major | Ab Major | Ab Major (2) |

TOP TIP: Although there are only three chords, you can see that there are four chords presented above. The reason is that chords don't have to be played from the name of the chord (root), any note can be in the bass of the chord. This is called an inversion. All major chords consist of 3 notes; the root, the third and the fifth. The 3rd and 5th come from the scale of the chord.

CONTINUE OVERLEAF...

Red Red Wine

SUGGESTED CHORD RHYTHM & SONG STRUCTURE

WATCH - LISTEN - PLAY ALONG!

SONG STRUCTURE

verse - verse - bridge - verse - instrumental break - bridge - verse - bridge - verse

VERSE

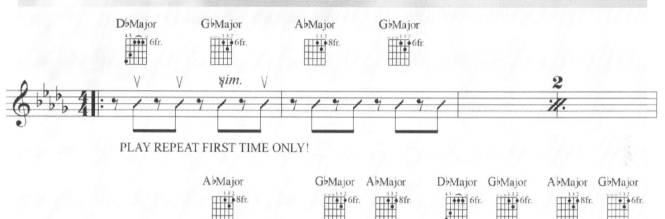

PLAY REPEAT FIRST TIME ONLY!

PLAY INSTRUMENT BREAK
INSTEAD AFTER FIRST TIME

BRIDGE

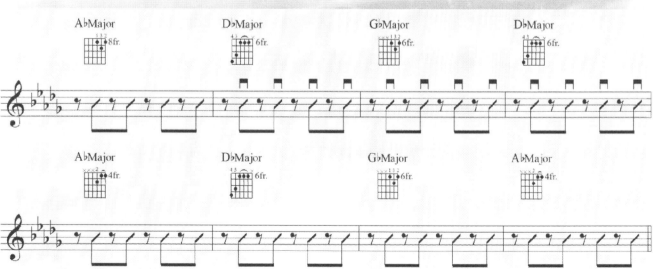

53

Red Red Wine

SUGGESTED CHORD RHYTHM & SONG STRUCTURE

WATCH - LISTEN - PLAY ALONG!

SONG STRUCTURE

verse - verse - bridge - verse - instrumental break - bridge
- verse - bridge - verse

INSTRUMENTAL BREAK

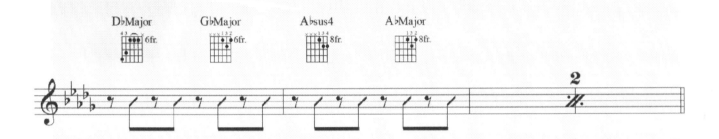

WHAT IS THIS I SEE BEFORE ME, A FOURTH CHORD?!

We have tried to ensure that all songs presented in this book actually only contain three chords in each song, just like our other songbook "22 songs just 2 chords per song" only has two chords in each song. It's not a case of you being presented with and playing "watered down" versions of songs that can still sound a bit like the original with only three chords.

In Red Red Wine we got to the end of the recording and discovered that for some bizarre reason the guitarist in UB40 decided to play a different chord that is not played at any other point in the track including within exactly the same chord sequence in earlier sections. However, this chord is there and the different chord is A flat sus4 which is shown above.

Instead of ignoring it we have included it for accuracies sake, however, it should be noted that you can just play an A flat Major chord and the song will sound absolutely fine.

SONG STRUCTURE

verse - verse - bridge - verse - instrumental break - bridge - verse - bridge - verse

Royals

- **Artist: Lorde**
- **Released: 2013**

NOTES: A truly stupendously popular song that has had over eight hundred million views on Youtube such is it's appeal.

This was the incredible debut single from New Zealand artist Lorde which has gone on to top the charts right across the entire globe. Now it's your turn to play it which you should find not that taxing. Remember to take head of the "TOP TIPS" as detailed below for the most effective rendering of this amazing electro pop song.

WATCH - LISTEN - PLAY ALONG!

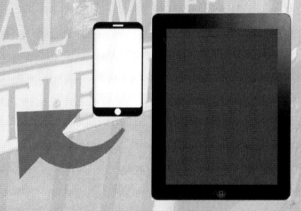

THE 3 CHORDS USED

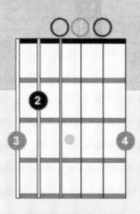

G Major

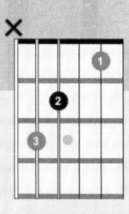

C Major

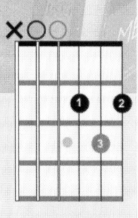

D Major

TOP TIPS: This song is very much synth. based but that does not mean that you can't play along and sound great doing so!

Make sure you build up the song from verse to pre chorus to chorus. Start by just playing the 4th thickest string as in the song, then move onto playing chords as the song builds in intensity.

CONTINUE OVERLEAF...

Royals

SUGGESTED CHORD RHYTHM & SONG STRUCTURE

WATCH - LISTEN - PLAY ALONG!

SONG STRUCTURE

Intro - verse - pre chorus - chorus - verse - pre chorus - chorus - bridge - chorus

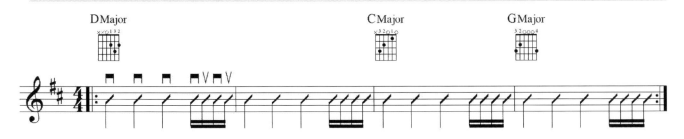

SONG STRUCTURE

The entire song is constructed out of the four bars shown above. The various parts of the song play the four bars a certain number of times.

Introduction 12 bars of a "D" note (each bar gets 4 beats)

Verse - "D" note only (open string 4) - Eight bars

Pre Chorus x 2

Chorus x 2

Verse - "D" note only (open string 4) - Eight bars

Pre Chorus x 2

Chorus x 2

Bridge x 2

Chorus x 2

Seven Bridges Road

- Artist: Eagles
- Released: 1980

NOTES: This song was penned by American singer/songwriter Steve Young and is so popular it must be up there with one of the most re-recorded songs ever. At least twenty two other artists have recorded this song which will have made Steve a very wealthy man indeed when we consider that other artists to record it include Dolly Parton, Joan Baez and Rita Coolidge.

This version of the song was recorded by the Eagles and it's not a video of a performance, but a video of a high quality recording (with images) if you know what we mean. Enjoy this great song!

WATCH - LISTEN - PLAY ALONG!

THE 3 CHORDS USED

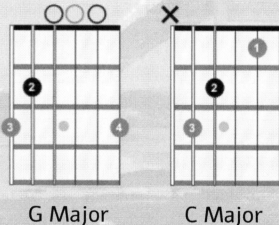

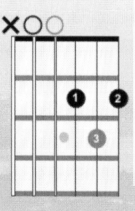

G Major   C Major   D Major

TOP TIPS: At the beginning and the end of the song the Eagles sing a cappella which means without instruments.

You can add the guitar part if you want or sing along and then bring the guitar in and leave it out at the appropriate time.

CONTINUE OVERLEAF...

Seven Bridges Road

SUGGESTED CHORD RHYTHM & SONG STRUCTURE

WATCH - LISTEN - PLAY ALONG!

SONG STRUCTURE

Intro; a cappella - verse - verse - outro; a cappella

INTRO (singing only (a cappella)) then play guitar chords before then playing the verse at bottom (guitar and vocal).

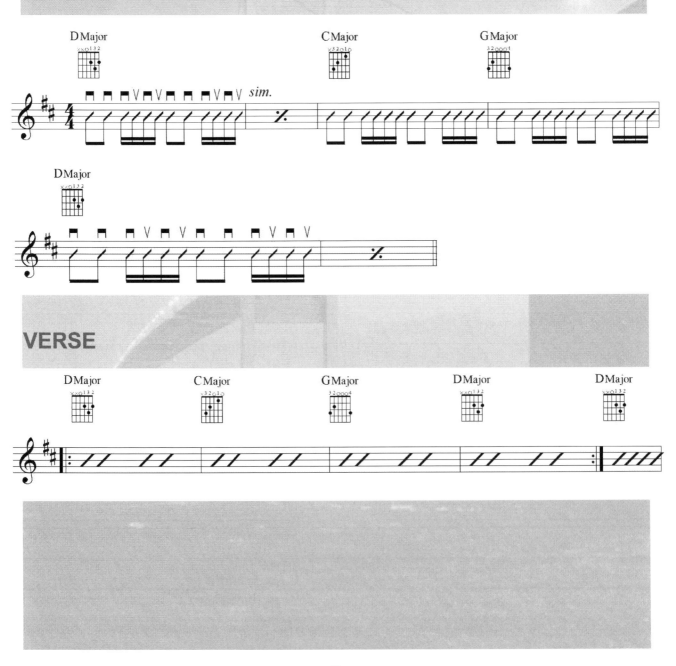

VERSE

Seven Bridges Road

SUGGESTED CHORD RHYTHM & SONG STRUCTURE

WATCH - LISTEN - PLAY ALONG!

SONG STRUCTURE

Intro; a cappella - verse - verse - outro; a cappella

VERSE CONTINUED

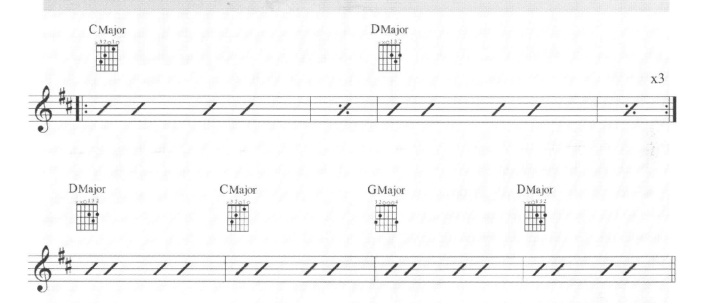

Back to the a cappella (singing only section) at the beginning.

SONG STRUCTURE
Intro; a cappella - verse - verse - outro; a cappella

Shake It Off

- Artist: Taylor Swift
- Released: 2014

NOTES: It's hard to overstate the incredible marketing work that has elevated Taylor Swift to the heights she now enjoys as a singer/songwriter. This song "Shake It Off" has had nearly three billion views on Youtube; a near impossibly large number to comprehend. The song itself has won a slew of awards and nominations yet at it's core it only has three chords.

As the song is predominantly drum and bass with synth sounds the guitar part is only representative of what is played, however, for singing along with a guitar...why not!

WATCH - LISTEN - PLAY ALONG!

THE 3 CHORDS USED

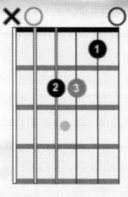

A minor

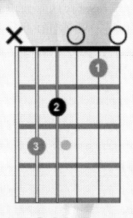
C Major

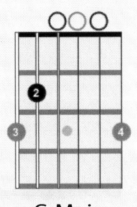
G Major

TOP TIPS: The song repeats the same chord progression throughout. The only thing that actually changes is at the beginning there is a really punchy a "syncopated" rhythmic part.

When the song moves to the chorus, simply move into an eighth rhythm in chorus.

CONTINUE OVERLEAF...

Shake It Off

SUGGESTED CHORD RHYTHM & SONG STRUCTURE

WATCH - LISTEN - PLAY ALONG!

SONG STRUCTURE

Intro - verse - pre chorus - chorus - verse - pre chorus - chorus - interlude - refrain till end

VERSE & PRE CHORUS

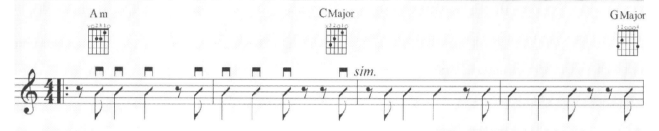

CHORUS

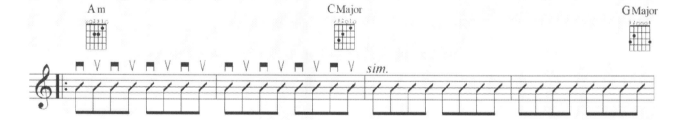

SONG STRUCTURE

Intro - verse - pre chorus - chorus - verse - pre chorus - interlude - refrain till end

Sweet Home Alabama

- ●Artist: Lynyrd Skynyrd
- ●Released: 1974

NOTES: Although none of the band were actually from Alabama, this didn't stop their song from becoming a massive world wide hit and shooting Lynyrd Skynyrd to stardom.

The song as given here just outlines the chords, however, on the next page you will see a suggested rhythm for the song. The first beat can be played by just playing the D string and not the chord. You'll find that by doing this simple thing, the piece sounds much more like the original riff based idea.

WATCH - LISTEN - PLAY ALONG!

THE 3 CHORDS USED

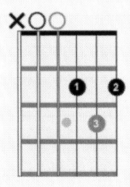

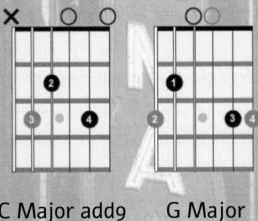

D Major   C Major add9   G Major

TOP TIP: The C Major add 9 chord is a C chord with an added note played by the pinky. Remember, this is not a new chord, just a changed chord you already know.

The G Major chord in this song uses four fingers. It's the same G Major chord but with the doubling of a note it makes the chord sound a bit more rocky and thicker in sound.

CONTINUE OVERLEAF...

Sweet Home Alabama

SUGGESTED CHORD RHYTHM & SONG STRUCTURE

WATCH - LISTEN - PLAY ALONG!

SONG STRUCTURE

Intro - verse - riff - verse - chorus - riff - verse - chorus -gtr. solo - verse - chorus

INTRO & VERSE

D Major   A Major

CHORUS & SOLO SECTION

D Major   A Major

SONG STRUCTURE

Intro - verse - riff - verse - chorus - riff - verse - chorus - gtr. solo - verse - chorus

The First Cut Is The Deepest

- ●Artist: Sheryl Crow
- ●Released: 2003

NOTES: Originally written by Cat Stevens back in 1969, this song has seen many re releases by a wide array of artists. In this instance you will be learning the Sheryl Crow version which features the all American girl "hanging out" in what looks like a mountainous desert area and riding horses whilst playing a guitar...a truly extended cowgirl advert if ever there was one.

Reaching number one in the UK, Netherlands and Germany, this song is probably most associated with Rod Stewart but Cat Stevens (born Steven Demetre Georgiou and now named Yusuf Islam) will not really be that bothered re ongoing royalty payments.

WATCH - LISTEN - PLAY ALONG!

THE 3 CHORDS USED

D Major

A Major

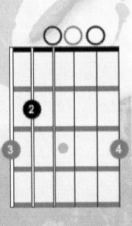

G Major

TOP TIPS: The opening or intro includes a Dsus4 chord. We didn't include it as we wanted to keep this song to three chords. This extra chord is very briefly used twice at the beginning so look it up but it's brief in it's use.

CONTINUE OVERLEAF...

The First Cut Is The Deepest

SUGGESTED CHORD RHYTHM & SONG STRUCTURE

WATCH - LISTEN - PLAY ALONG!

SONG STRUCTURE

Intro - verse - chorus - verse - chorus - gtr. solo - verse - chorus - outro

INTRO

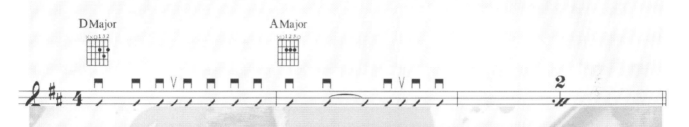

VERSE

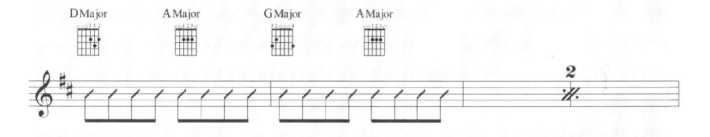

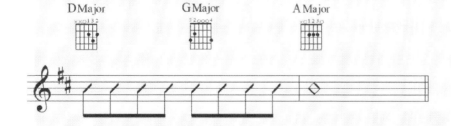

CONTINUE OVERLEAF...

The First Cut Is The Deepest

SUGGESTED CHORD RHYTHM & SONG STRUCTURE

WATCH - LISTEN - PLAY ALONG!

SONG STRUCTURE

Intro - verse - chorus - verse - chorus - gtr. solo - verse - chorus - outro

CHORUS

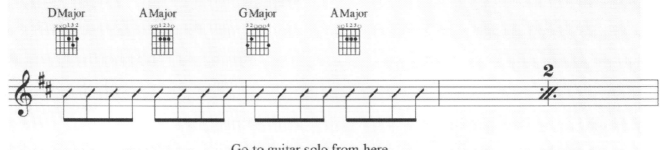

Go to guitar solo from here at end of second chorus

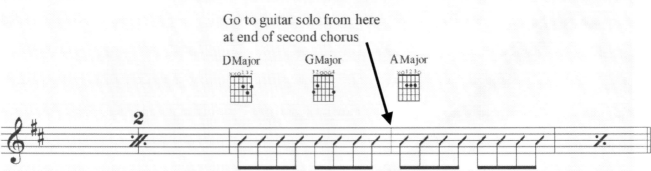

GUITAR SOLO SEQUENCE

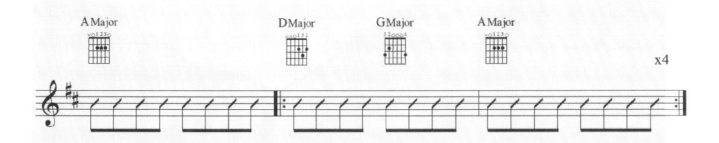

x4

CONTINUE OVERLEAF...

The First Cut Is The Deepest

SUGGESTED CHORD RHYTHM & SONG STRUCTURE

WATCH - LISTEN - PLAY ALONG!

SONG STRUCTURE

Intro - verse - chorus - verse - chorus - gtr. solo - verse - chorus - outro

CHORUS & OUTRO

CONTINUE OVERLEAF…

The First Cut Is The Deepest

SUGGESTED CHORD RHYTHM & SONG STRUCTURE

WATCH - LISTEN - PLAY ALONG!

SONG STRUCTURE

Intro - verse - chorus - verse - chorus - gtr. solo - verse - chorus - outro

CHORUS & OUTRO

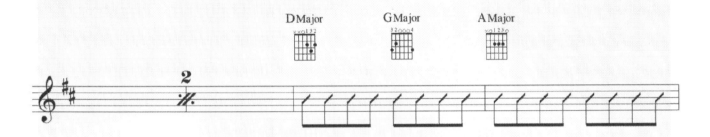

SONG STRUCTURE

Intro - verse - chorus - verse - chorus - gtr. solo - verse - chorus - outro

The Tide Is High

- **Artist: Blondie**
- **Released: 1980**

NOTES: Yet another song that became a hit but not for the original artist who penned it. Reggae singer/songwriter John Holt of the Paragons wrote the song in 1967 but it was not until the group Blondie with singer Debbie Harry leading that the song became a hit.

As the song arrangement is heavily influenced by it's original reggae roots the guitar work is all played "off the beat". That is, when you tap your foot along to a song you are playing "on the beat". Playing off the beat would be when between foot taps your foot is at the highest point before returning to the ground.

WATCH - LISTEN - PLAY ALONG!

THE 3 CHORDS USED

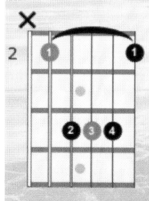

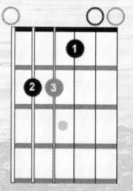

B Major   E Major   F# Major

TOP TIP: The song Barbara Ann is loosely based around the blues progression and as such, it's a great song to learn because thousands of other songs use a similar sequence of chords (usually in other key centres).

To play this song you need to NOT PLAY at times! Listen to the track via the QR code above and notice how many times the instruments are NOT playing. Learning when not to play will add excitement when you do re-enter.

CONTINUE OVERLEAF...

The Tide Is High

SUGGESTED CHORD RHYTHM & SONG STRUCTURE

WATCH - LISTEN - PLAY ALONG!

SONG STRUCTURE

Intro - verse - chorus - verse - chorus - brass instrumental -
verse - chorus^X - chorus^Y - brass outro till end

INTRO, VERSE, BRASS INST., BRASS OUTRO

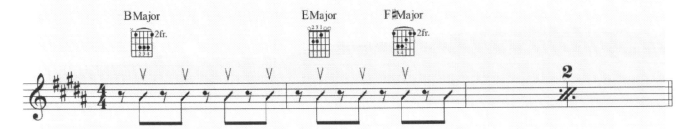

CHORUS

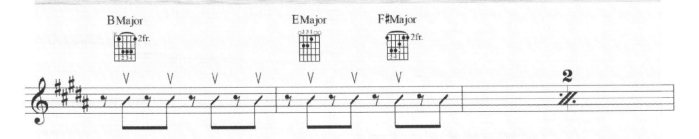

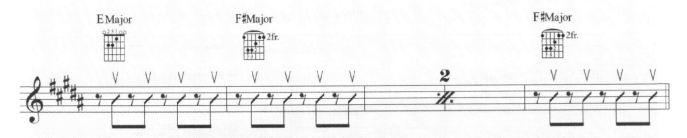

SONG STRUCTURE

Intro - verse - chorus - verse - chorus - brass instrumental - verse - chorus^X - chorus^Y - brass outro till end

Note: Intro, verse, brass instrumental and brass outro all use the same chord sequence as shown at top of page.

NOTE: Chorus^X = 2nd line of chorus Emaj - F#Maj x3, Chorus^Y = As Intro.

The Joker

- **Artist: Steve Miller Band**
- **Released: 1973**

NOTES: This song is an example of how advertising can re ignite interest in a piece of music and that a great song never goes out of fashion. Originally hitting the highest heights in America in 1973, this song got to number one in the UK charts in 1990 due to it's being used in a jeans TV advert.

The three chords used are all barre chords. The C Major chord could have been played as an open string chord, however, this is quite a rock sounding song so the barre chord lower strings give the sound a bit of oomph!

WATCH - LISTEN - PLAY ALONG!

THE 3 CHORDS USED

F Major

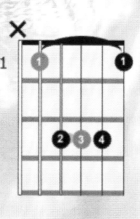

Bb Major

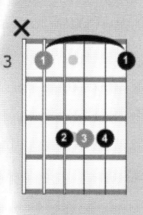

C Major

TOP TIPS: As mentioned above, the barre chords give a much more powerful rock inspired sound than open chords.

Try playing just the lowest 3 notes of a barre chord if you want to really make the chord sound "heavy".

These chords btw are called "power" chords or sometimes known as "5" chords as in F5, Bb5 and C5 as it would be in this song.

CONTINUE OVERLEAF...

The Joker

SUGGESTED CHORD RHYTHM & SONG STRUCTURE

WATCH - LISTEN - PLAY ALONG!

SONG STRUCTURE

verse - chorus - guitar solo interlude 1 - verse - chorus - guitar solo interlude 2 - verse - refrain till end

VERSE & GUITAR SOLO INTERLUDE 1

NOTES: (music x 4 for 1st verse, x 2 for guitar solo interlude, x 2 for 2nd verse)

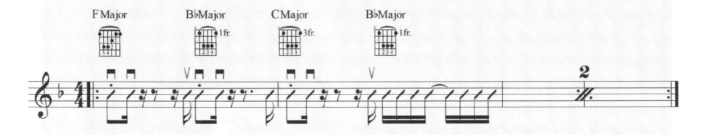

CHORUS & GUITAR SOLO INTERLUDE 2

NOTES: After playing verse 2 as shown above, again play the chorus as shown below but take the first time ending BOTH times. <u>Do not</u> play the 2nd time ending after verse 2.

The chorus is used for the guitar solo interlude after chorus two has been sung.

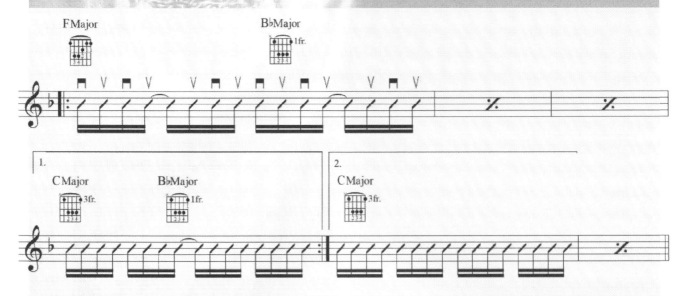

SONG STRUCTURE

Verse - chorus - guitar solo interlude 1 - verse - chorus - guitar solo interlude 2 - verse - refrain till end

Walk Of Life

- **Artist: Dire Straights**
- **Released: 1985**

NOTES: Dire Straights biggest money making song in the USA. This three chord wonder is instantly recognisable whenever it's played. These three chords have been used in countless songs and blues progressions, yet such is the talent of the songwriter Mark Knopfler, they still make a song that is catchy and loved by millions.

Being able to confidently play these three chords both independently of each other and together in a chord sequence will mean you'll also be able to play thousands of other songs based on these three same chords!

WATCH - LISTEN - PLAY ALONG!

THE 3 CHORDS USED

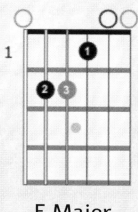

E Major

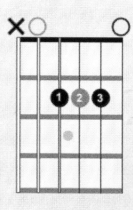

A Major

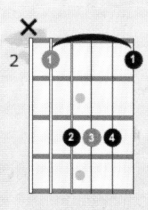

B Major

TOP TIPS: Try looking at the finger position within each chord and what it actually has to do to move to the next chord.

For example, if you look at E major you will see that the second and third finger are in exactly the same position as they are when playing the A major chord. Lesson learnt...look for fingers that move as a team and keep them together for quicker movement between chords.

CONTINUE OVERLEAF...

Walk Of Life

SUGGESTED CHORD RHYTHM & SONG STRUCTURE

WATCH - LISTEN - PLAY ALONG!

SONG STRUCTURE

Intro - verse - chorus - refrain x 1 - verse - chorus - refrain x 2 - verse - refrain till end

INTRO & REFRAIN

play rhythm as verse when playing the interlude

VERSE

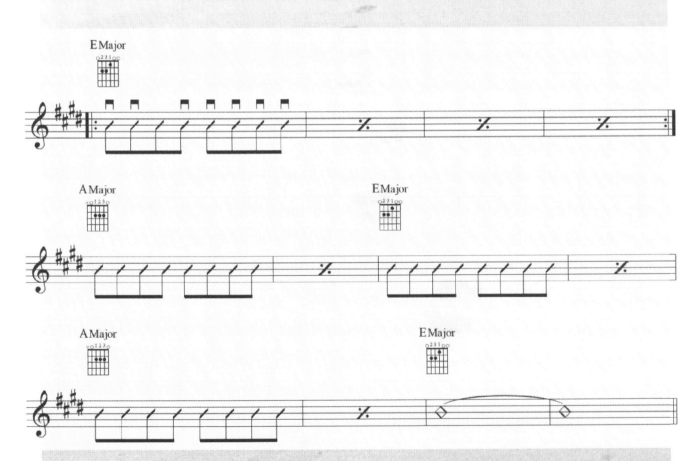

CONTINUE OVERLEAF...

Walk Of Life

SUGGESTED CHORD RHYTHM & SONG STRUCTURE

WATCH - LISTEN - PLAY ALONG!

SONG STRUCTURE

Intro - verse - chorus - refrain x 1 - verse - chorus - refrain x 2 - verse - refrain till end

CHORUS

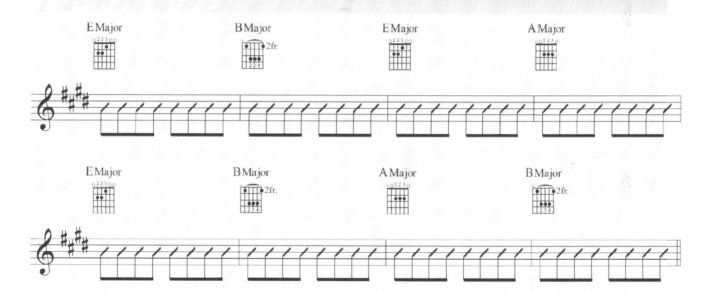

SONG STRUCTURE

Intro - verse - chorus - refrain x 1 - verse - chorus - refrain x 2 - verse - refrain till end

Walk On The Wild Side

- **Artist: Lou Reed**
- **Released: 1972**

NOTES: Just so you know the company that Lou Reed was keeping back in the early 70s, the album that this song came from was produced by non other than David Bowie and his then guitar sideman Mick Ronson!

One of the great songs that defined the decade of the 1970s, it introduced a wide range of taboo subjects in musical form and recorded which resulted in the song being censored in the United States on launch.

WATCH - LISTEN - PLAY ALONG!

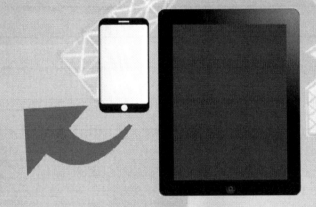

THE 3 CHORDS USED

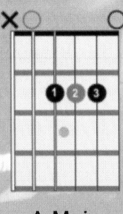

A Major

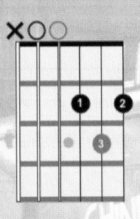

D Major

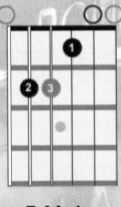

E Major

TOP TIPS: Little Ghost is all about the right hand rhythm playing (assuming your right handed that is) so take your time and work up the sound by using constant up and down strokes and missing out the hit on the strings whilst still making the action of your arm.

CONTINUE OVERLEAF...

Walk On The Wild Side

SUGGESTED CHORD RHYTHM & SONG STRUCTURE

WATCH - LISTEN - PLAY ALONG!

SONG STRUCTURE

Intro - verse - chorus - verse - chorus etc.

INTRO

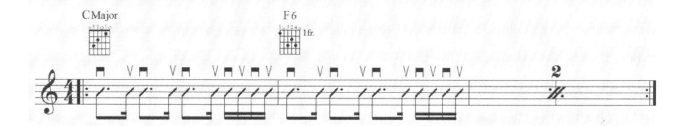

VERSE & CHORUS

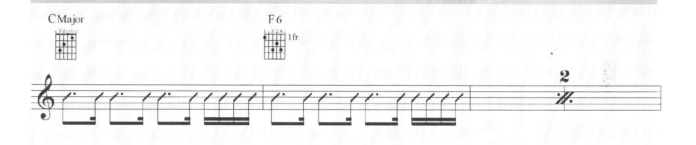

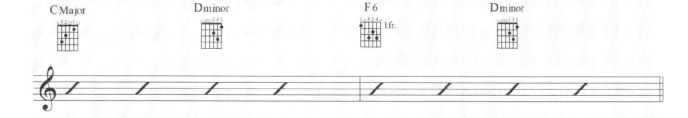

SONG STRUCTURE
After each verse and chorus, repeat the intro as an interlude.

What's Up?

- ●Artist: 4 Non Blondes
- ●Released: 1993

NOTES: This song by Linda Perry might have you thinking why is it called that as the title of the song is not the main refrain in the tune, however, this was deliberate in order to avoid confusion with the Marvin Gaye song "What's Going On?" released in 1971.

An amazing hit song that topped the charts not only in America but across Europe with oddly only the UK not registering a number one spot.

WATCH - LISTEN - PLAY ALONG!

THE 3 CHORDS USED

TOP TIPS: A simple song that's only real challenges are being able to play the B minor barre chord and to ensure that the song builds in intensity through your vocal and right hand rhythm playing.

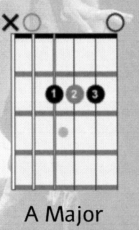

A Major

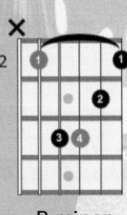

B minor

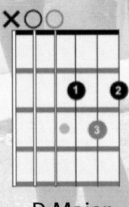

D Major

CONTINUE OVERLEAF...

What's Up?

SUGGESTED CHORD RHYTHM & SONG STRUCTURE

WATCH - LISTEN - PLAY ALONG!

SONG STRUCTURE

Intro - verse - pre chorus - chorus - solo section - verse - pre
chorus - chorus - refrain till end

INTRO, VERSE, PRE - CHORUS, CHORUS & SOLO SECTION

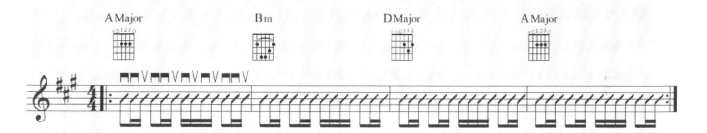

SONG STRUCTURE

Intro - verse - pre chorus - chorus - solo section - verse - pre
chorus - chorus - chorus - refrain till end

When You Say Nothing At All

- **Artist: Alison Krauss**
- **Released: 1995**

NOTES: This is one of those massive hit songs that you thought was originally performed by Ronan Keating for the film Notting Hill...but some of you would of course think, yes but it was Alison Krauss that originally recorded it and of course you would be wrong.

The original version of this song which was also a hit was released in 1988 by Keith Whitley who tragically passed away in 1989. The song was written and composed by Paul Overstreet and Don Schlitz. The Alison Krauss video has been watched nearly seventy million times and the other videos each have seen around the twenty million mark. An amazing song loved by millions around the world.

WATCH - LISTEN - PLAY ALONG!

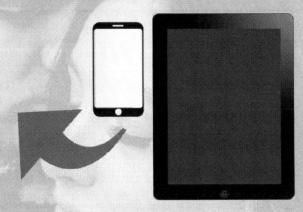

THE 3 MAIN CHORDS USED

TOP TIPS: You will definitely find these chords a challenge.

Keep working at it because when you do get these chords together they open up a new range of song possibilities. Play a simple picking pattern on these chords for best effect.

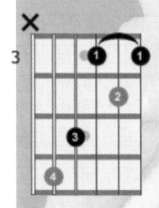

Eb Major

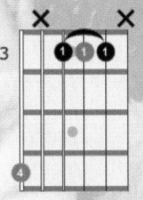

Bb Major

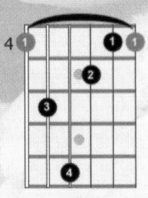

Ab Major add 9

CONTINUE OVERLEAF...

When You Say Nothing At All

SUGGESTED CHORD RHYTHM & SONG STRUCTURE

WATCH - LISTEN - PLAY ALONG!

SONG STRUCTURE

Intro - verse - chorus - Intro - verse - chorus - Gtr. Instrumental
- chorus - coda

INTRO.

VERSE 1 & 2

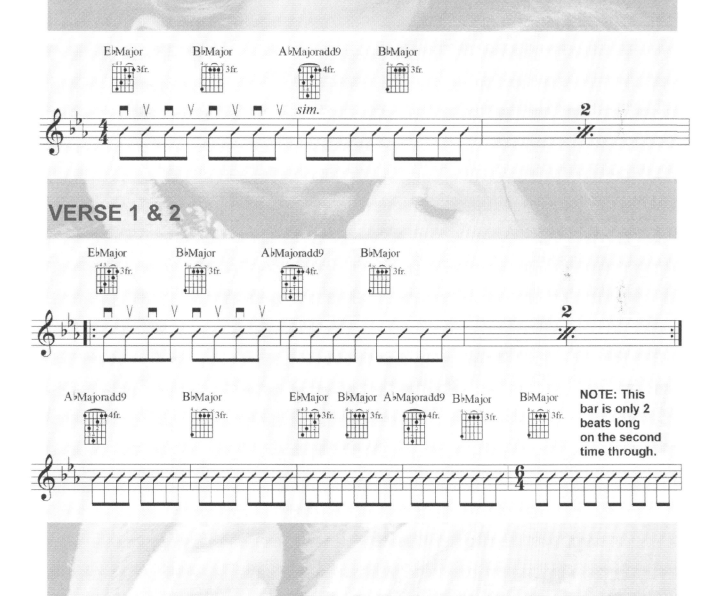

NOTE: This bar is only 2 beats long on the second time through.

CONTINUE OVERLEAF...

When You Say Nothing At All

SUGGESTED CHORD RHYTHM & SONG STRUCTURE

WATCH - LISTEN - PLAY ALONG!

SONG STRUCTURE

Intro - verse - chorus - Intro - verse - chorus - Gtr. Instrumental
- chorus - coda

CHORUS & INTERLUDE

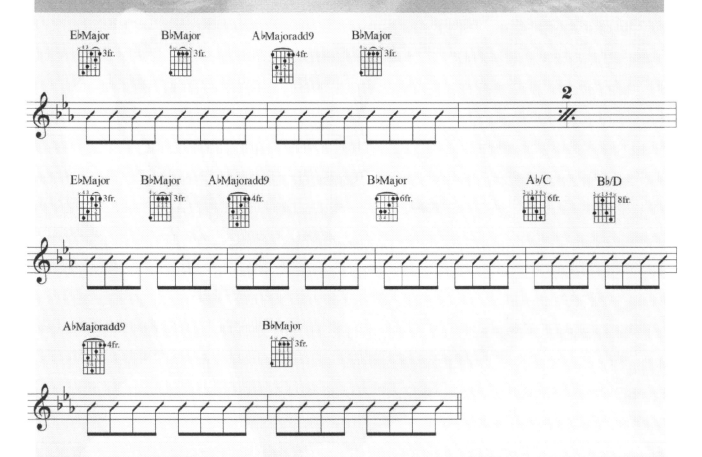

ALTERNATE CHORDS - You can play the Ab Major add 9 and the Bb Major chords as given at the start of the song instead of Ab/C and Bb/D. The alternate chords shown below suit the song really well but the last two are difficult to play.

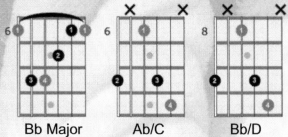

Bb Major   Ab/C   Bb/D

CONTINUE OVERLEAF...

When You Say Nothing At All

SUGGESTED CHORD RHYTHM & SONG STRUCTURE

WATCH - LISTEN - PLAY ALONG!

SONG STRUCTURE

Intro - verse - chorus - Intro - verse - chorus - Gtr. Instrumental - chorus - coda

GTR. INSTRUMENTAL

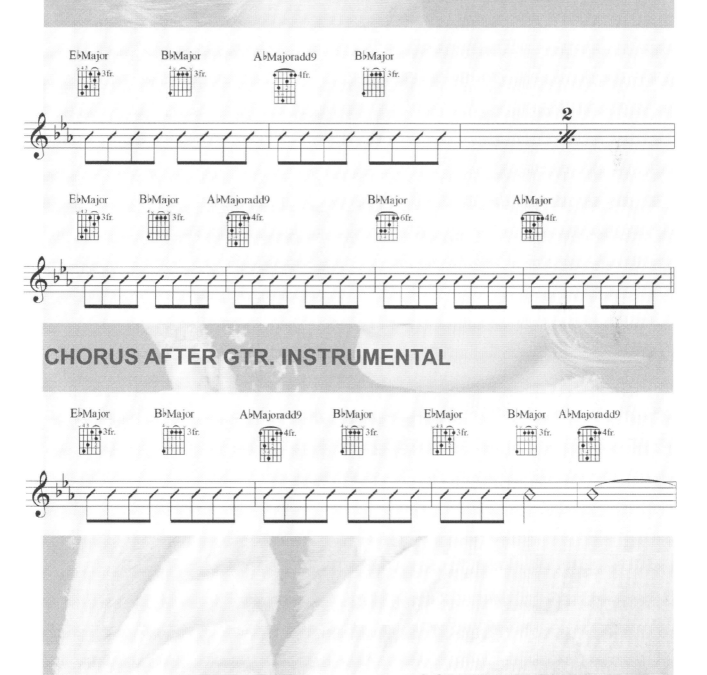

CHORUS AFTER GTR. INSTRUMENTAL

CONTINUE OVERLEAF...

When You Say Nothing At All

SUGGESTED CHORD RHYTHM & SONG STRUCTURE

WATCH - LISTEN - PLAY ALONG!

SONG STRUCTURE

Intro - verse - chorus - Intro - verse - chorus - Gtr. Instrumental - chorus - coda

FINAL CHORUS CONTINUED

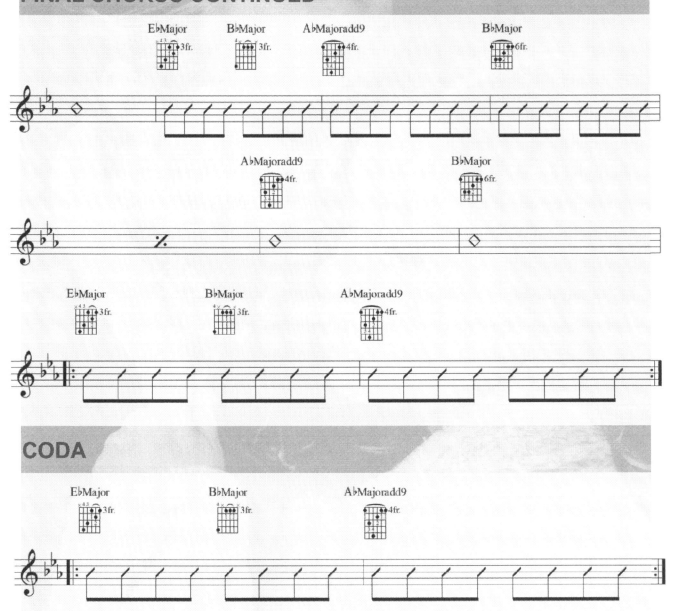

CODA

SONG STRUCTURE

Intro - verse - chorus - Intro - verse - chorus - Gtr. Instrumental - chorus - coda

Why'd You Only Call Me When You're High?

- Artist: Arctic Monkeys
- Released: 2013

NOTES: This song hit number one in the UK indie charts when released, although there was a leaked release (or miscommunication) which almost sunk the release. You'll be playing along with the bands live video version with the song proper coming in at twenty one seconds in.

WATCH - LISTEN - PLAY ALONG!

THE 3 CHORDS USED

E minor

C Major

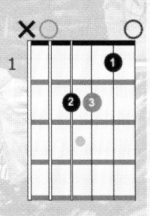

A minor

TOP TIPS: As this book is all about playing songs with the underlying chords in them there are no lead lines given. You should, however, listen to the opening of this song and see if you can work out the "riff" that the guitar plays at the opening which is actually based around these three chords.

CONTINUE OVERLEAF…

Why'd You Only Call Me When You're High?

SUGGESTED CHORD RHYTHM & SONG STRUCTURE

WATCH - LISTEN - PLAY ALONG!

SONG STRUCTURE

Intro - verse - chorus - verse - chorus - bridge - gtr. solo - outro

INTRO (after drums), VERSE, CHORUS

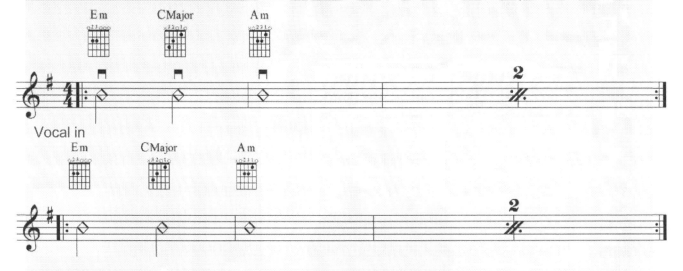

BRIDGE & (LAST LINE) GTR. SOLO & OUTRO

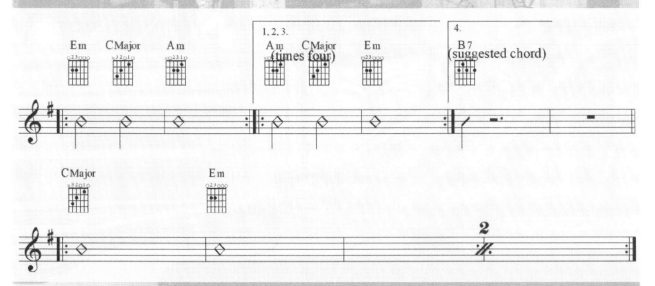

SONG STRUCTURE

Intro - verse - chorus - verse - chorus - bridge - gtr. solo - outro

Wonderful

- **Artist: Everclear**
- **Released: 2000**

NOTES: You may have heard the perhaps rather unkind phrase "one hit wonder" said about specific artists and bands; well in this case it's probably true. This has been Everclear's only hit to date but with over eight million views racked up on Youtube and a song that hit number one in Canada and made top ten in a slew of American charts. Everclear are best defined by the amazing person that is Art Alexakis who is still the bands main singer.

As much as the song was popular, the video was also a big hit and is definitely worth watching before you start learning to play along.

WATCH - LISTEN - PLAY ALONG!

THE 3 CHORDS USED

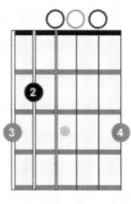

G Major

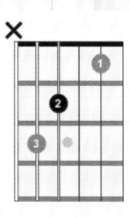

C Major

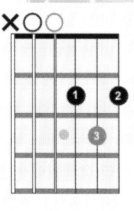

D Major

TOP TIPS: Nothing much to say about this easy and fun to play song other than at one point in the song the bass line goes down from G to F# to E. When the E is played in the bass, you are still playing a G Major chord. For the theory buffs this technically means you are playing an Em7 chord.

CONTINUE OVERLEAF...

Wonderful

SUGGESTED CHORD RHYTHM & SONG STRUCTURE

WATCH - LISTEN - PLAY ALONG!

SONG STRUCTURE

Intro - verse 1 - chorus 1 - verse 2 - chorus 2 - chorus 3 - outro

INTRO

VERSE 1 and 2

x4 on 1st verse
x2 on 2nd verse

CHORUS 1 and 2

x1 on 1st chorus
x2 on 2nd chorus

CONTINUE OVERLEAF…

Wonderful

SUGGESTED CHORD RHYTHM & SONG STRUCTURE

WATCH - LISTEN - PLAY ALONG!

SONG STRUCTURE

Intro - verse 1 - chorus 1 - verse 2 - chorus 2 - chorus 3 - outro

CHORUS 3

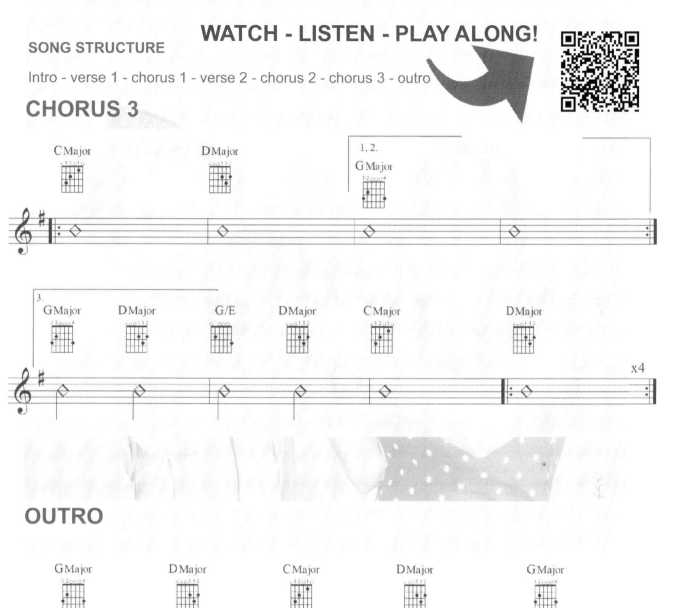

OUTRO

SONG STRUCTURE

Intro - verse 1 - chorus 1 - verse 2 - chorus 2 - chorus 3 - outro

Werewolves of London

- **Artist: Warren Zevon**
- **Released: 1978**

NOTES: Who would have thought that a song that sounds as straight forward as this one and which has a very repetitive construction (form) would apparently cause so many problems in the studio but it did. The recording of this song took so long that it ate up the vast majority of the whole albums budget!

Warren Zevon was a prolific song writers and this song was just one of many songs that he composed throughout his life. Sadly Warren died in 2003 at the relatively young age of just fifty six years old.

WATCH - LISTEN - PLAY ALONG!

THE 3 CHORDS USED

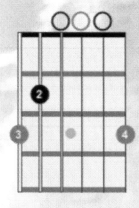

G Major

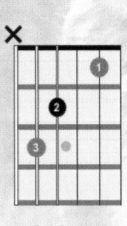

C Major

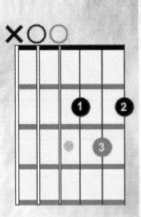

D Major

TOP TIPS: Another great song to learn where the repetitive nature of the chords and the simple form means you can really concentrate on the right hand re your rhythm playing.

Study the down and up strokes carefully at the beginning of the song.

CONTINUE OVERLEAF...

Werewolves of London

SUGGESTED CHORD RHYTHM & SONG STRUCTURE

WATCH - LISTEN - PLAY ALONG!

SONG STRUCTURE

Intro - verse - chorus - verse - chorus - gtr. solo - verse - chorus - verse - chorus

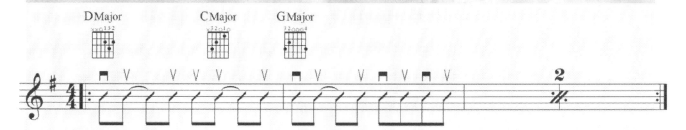

SONG STRUCTURE

The entire song is constructed out of the four bars shown above. The various parts of the song play the four bars a certain number of times.

Introduction x 2

Verse x 2

Chorus x 2

Verse x 2

Chorus x 2

Guitar solo x 2

Verse x 2

Chorus x 2

Verse x 3

Chorus x 2

18 Candles

- ●Artist: Nina Nesbitt
- ●Released: 2014

NOTES: This Scottish pop singer really smashed into the public's consciousness with this two thousand and fourteen song which is, well all about age which would seem to suggest that she thinks she won't make it past thirty six; an age so ancient at eighteen that it probably seems a lifetime away.

As part of the album "Peroxide", Nina suitably died her hair peroxide blonde for the outing of this work, she hit number one in the Scottish chart as well as eleven in the UK and forty in the Irish charts.

WATCH - LISTEN - PLAY ALONG!

THE 3 CHORDS USED

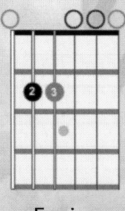

E minor

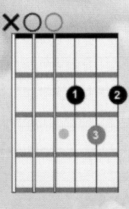

D Major

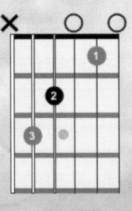

C Major

TOP TIPS: One of the reasons we were drawn to include this song is, apart from it sounding great, the video being crystal clear is that it is in a minor key!

Sometimes three chord minor key songs are hard to find...

CONTINUE OVERLEAF...

18 Candles

SUGGESTED CHORD RHYTHM & SONG STRUCTURE

WATCH - LISTEN - PLAY ALONG!

SONG STRUCTURE

Intro - verse - verse - chorus - verse - verse

- chorus - extended intro version - chorus till end

INTRO

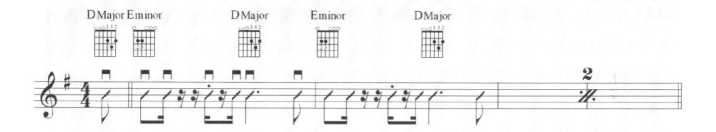

VERSE

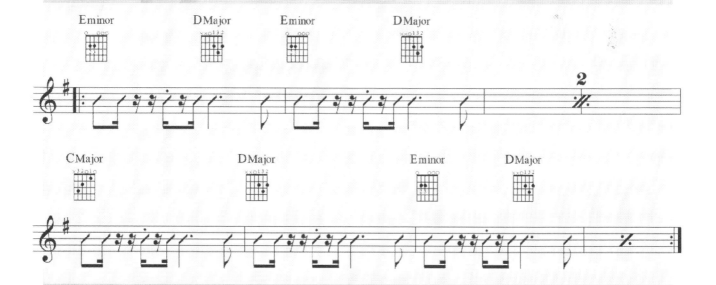

CONTINUE OVERLEAF...

18 Candles

SUGGESTED CHORD RHYTHM & SONG STRUCTURE

WATCH - LISTEN - PLAY ALONG!

SONG STRUCTURE

Intro - verse - verse - chorus - verse - verse

- chorus - extended intro version - chorus till end

CHORUS

C Major   D Major   E minor

INTRO

VERSE

VERSE

CHORUS

INTRO LINE x3 with an added one bar drum break at end

CHORUS R&R till end

SONG STRUCTURE

Intro - verse - verse - chorus - verse - verse - chorus - extended intro section - chorus till end

APPENDICES

1. A lead sheet which defines common musical notation to help you better understand the musical and symbols found within this book.

2. A rhythm tree to help you gain a deeper understanding of rhythmic notation.

LEAD SHEET

All Brassed Up

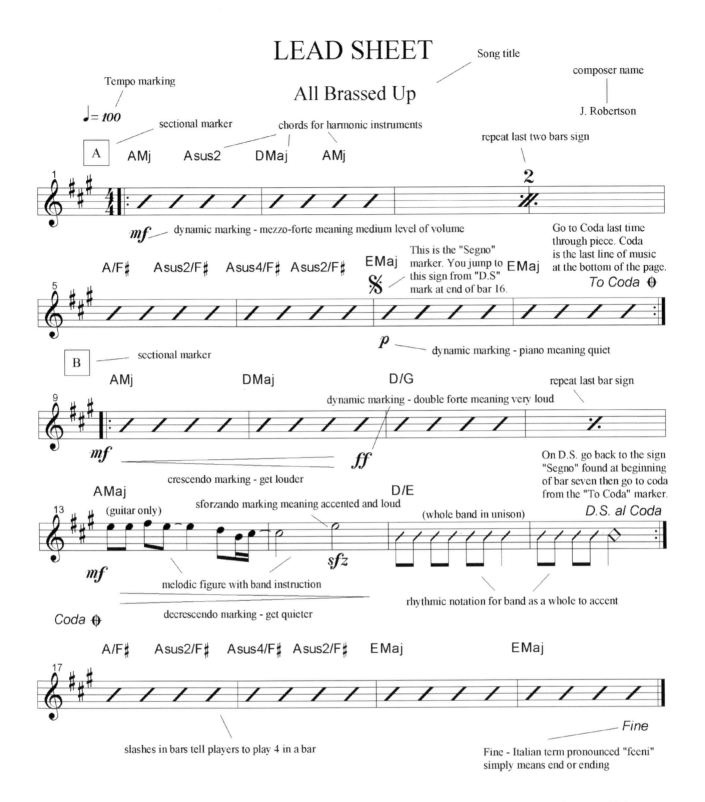

FORM - The Form is AABB; each section being titled A or B. Last time through from bar 16 take DS which means jump straight to bar 7 where the S with the slash and dots are (segno), then at the end of bar 8 take the CODA by jumping straight to bar 17 to the end of the song.

RHYTHMIC NOTATION

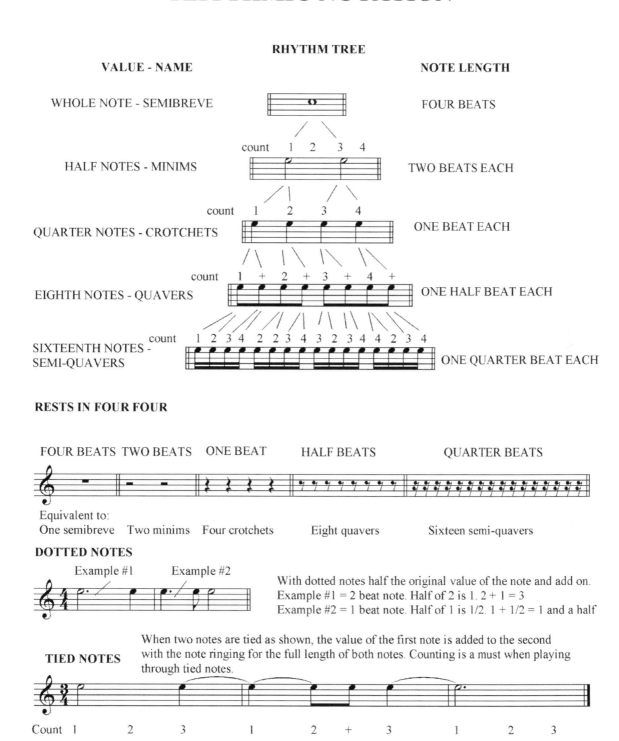

RHYTHM TREE

VALUE - NAME

NOTE LENGTH

WHOLE NOTE - SEMIBREVE — FOUR BEATS

count 1 2 3 4

HALF NOTES - MINIMS — TWO BEATS EACH

count 1 2 3 4

QUARTER NOTES - CROTCHETS — ONE BEAT EACH

count 1 + 2 + 3 + 4 +

EIGHTH NOTES - QUAVERS — ONE HALF BEAT EACH

count 1 2 3 4 2 2 3 4 3 2 3 4 4 2 3 4

SIXTEENTH NOTES - SEMI-QUAVERS — ONE QUARTER BEAT EACH

RESTS IN FOUR FOUR

FOUR BEATS | TWO BEATS | ONE BEAT | HALF BEATS | QUARTER BEATS

Equivalent to:
One semibreve   Two minims   Four crotchets   Eight quavers   Sixteen semi-quavers

DOTTED NOTES

Example #1   Example #2

With dotted notes half the original value of the note and add on.
Example #1 = 2 beat note. Half of 2 is 1. 2 + 1 = 3
Example #2 = 1 beat note. Half of 1 is 1/2. 1 + 1/2 = 1 and a half

TIED NOTES

When two notes are tied as shown, the value of the first note is added to the second with the note ringing for the full length of both notes. Counting is a must when playing through tied notes.

Count   1   2   3   1   2   +   3   1   2   3

GET THE GMI COMPANION BOOK ON AMAZON AND ALL GOOD BOOKSTORES ONLINE AND AT GMI!

Hopefully you've had a great time learning some of the biggest hits in popular music history, but you don't need to stop here.

Our best selling companion book features, yes you've guess it, 22 hit songs just 2 chords per song!

You can get the printed wire comb bound flat lie version of our books direct from our website shop at https://gmiguitarshop.com as well as a large selection of free aids and lesson for guitarists.

Learn to play the songs of the Beatles, Eurythmics, Arctic Monkeys, The Mavericks, Oasis, Robin Thicke, Billy Ray Cyrus, Eric Clapton, U2, Nirvana, Mary J Blige, Fleetwood Mac, Chic, Bruno Mars, America, Jane's Addiction, Maroon 5, Bruce Springsteen, Sublime, The Doors, Ne-Yo, Alicia Keys in no time at all!

JUST A SMALL SELECTION OF OTHER GREAT TITLES AVAILABLE FROM GMI - Guitar & Music Institute

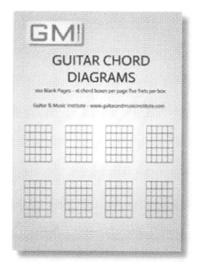

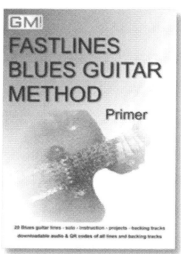

ALL OUR PRINTED TITLES CAN BE PURCHASED FROM AMAZON AND ALL GOOD ONLINE BOOK SELLERS. VISIT GMIGUITARSHOP.COM FOR DOWNLOAD ALTERNATIVES

CHECK OUT GMI - GUITAR & MUSIC INSTITUTE ON THE WEB!

GMI has been creating the best in guitar articles, gear reviews, podcasts, guitar lessons, guitar publications, and a host of E-learning products for guitarists around the world since 2013.

Check out our website and get your hands on all our free content, free lessons and a huge range of resources for guitarists of all ages, styles and abilities. Also, look us up on Youtube!

https://www.guitarandmusicinstitute.com

DOWNLOAD THE FREE PRACTICE TRACKS & EXAMPLE RHYTHM TRACKS THAT ACCOMPANY THIS BOOK.

Each of the songs in this book have practice tracks to help you get the chord changes together quicker as well as demonstration practice tracks of the rhythms shown in each song.

NOTE: The total size of the WINRAR file is 331 megabytes.

Point a QR code reader at the box above to download

OR copy and past the following URL in your browser:

https://gmiguitarshop.com/products/practice-tracks-for-learn-33-hit-songs-on-guitar-just-3-chords-per-song-the-beginners-guitar-favourite?_pos=2&_sid=46fc5e752&_ss=r

OR go to:

https://gmiguitarshop.com and search for "33 hit songs" (no quote marks) and look for practice tracks.

We offer guitarists of all styles, ages and technical abilities free resources to download from our online store at https://gmiguitarshop.com

Come on over and download as much of our free content as well as viewing our other online offerings.

Printed in Great Britain
by Amazon